GET YOUR BONUS

THE DIGITAL VERSION OF "PLANT BASED COOKBOOK" BY MELISSA JEFFERSON IS 100% FREE. YOU DON'T NEED TO ENTER ANY DETAILS EXCEPT YOUR NAME AND EMAIL ADDRESS.

PLANT BASED COOKBOOK

Tasty and Easy Plant-Based Recipes to Boost Your Well-Being, Improve your Energy, and Feel Lighter

To download your bonus scan the QR code below or go to

https://bonus4books.com/melinda-jefferson-md

SCAN ME

TABLE OF CONTENTS

5	INTRODUCTION
14	BREAKFAST
23	BEANS, RICE & GRAINS
31	PASTA & COUSCOUS
41	MEAT
50	FISH & SEAFOOD
59	SALADS & VEGETABLES
66	SNACKS & APPETIZERS
72	JUICE & SMOOTHIES
77	DESSERTS
86	12-WEEK MEAL PLAN
93	CONCLUSION
94	INDEX

INTRODUCTION

MEDITERRANEAN DIET FUNDAMENTALS	6
FOOD PYRAMID: WHAT IT IS AND HOW TO USE IT	8
MEDITERRANEAN DIET HEALTH BENEFITS	9
FAQ	12
WHAT TO EAT AND WHAT TO AVOID	13
Foods to Eat	*13*
Foods to Avoid	*15*

Mediterranean Diet Fundamentals

Mediterranean diet, as a popular diet, is often quoted as one of the healthiest and most wholesome. The Mediterranean one is an ideal lifestyle focusing on healthy foods and the pleasure of conviviality. So how does this diet work in improving our health?

The Mediterranean diet improves the lipid profile by lowering total cholesterol levels while simultaneously reducing LDL cholesterol levels and increasing HDL or good cholesterol levels.

The Mediterranean Diet is also helpful for weight control, as it provides sufficient fiber and low glycemic index carbohydrates that keep appetite under control for hours without causing blood sugar spikes or feelings of hunger soon after eating.

This regimen also helps prevent diabetes by providing the proper amounts of fiber, fats, and sugars that help to control blood sugar levels and insulin sensitivity. High blood sugar levels are often associated with diabetes and stroke, while low blood sugar levels are commonly seen in people with diabetes who do not consume enough fat or protein in their food. In addition, the Mediterranean diet contains sufficient amounts of omega-3 fatty acids, which are beneficial for reducing triglycerides, preventing heart disease, and lowering the risk of stroke. This makes the Mediterranean diet incredibly beneficial for people with diabetes as well.

Also, the Mediterranean Diet may help prevent Alzheimer's Disease by providing enough omega-3 fatty acids, essential for healthy brain cell membranes, and preventing the accumulation of beta-amyloid plaque in the brain.

The Mediterranean diet also contributes to a reduction in heart disease risk due to its focus on unsaturated fatty acids that are much healthier than saturated fat. Foods containing healthy fats include olive oil, which is rich in antioxidants called polyphenols, which are excellent for fighting cancer and heart disease by preventing cells from oxidizing or damaging themselves.

Doctors recommend the Mediterranean Diet because it is rich in antioxidants, fiber, omega-3 fatty acids, and polyphenols. The diet is also low in calories, with a healthy fat intake that helps to prevent weight gain.

The food of this dietary approach are packed with nutrients essential for good health, and most traditional recipes contain these key element —fruits, vegetables, nuts, and seeds. As a result, the diet has been proven to be one of the healthiest and most wholesome. In short, the Mediterranean one is a healthy eating approach that involves moderation in overall calories required for energy consumption while at the same time providing essential elements needed for good health, which include fibers, omega-3 fatty acids, and polyphenols—all necessary nutrients required for human health.

Some of the Main Principles of The Mediterranean Diet Include:

1. Cook From Scratch and Avoid Processed Food

When you are making something from scratch, it tastes better. When you know what is in your food, it feels good to eat. Eating fresh foods is also more nutritious than processed foods because they have the most nutrients still intact.

2. Eat Foods That Are Fresh and In Season

Eating what is in season is a very good idea. That way, your body can take advantage of the nutrients that are available to you during certain times of the year.

3. Eat Mostly Fish and Beans, but Have Eggs and Chicken Too

A healthy diet should include mostly fish and beans, with some eggs or chicken for variety.

4. To Get Energy, Eat Whole Grains and Potatoes

Grains and potatoes have a lot of energy. They are very nutritious and will help you feel full throughout the day.

5. Eat Some Cheese Every Day. Cheese from Sheep and Goat Is Good

Cheese is a good source of calcium and protein. Cheese from sheep or goats is considered to be the healthiest because they are lower in fat.

6. Eat A Little Bit of Red Meat and Mix It with Other Foods

The nutrients in red meat are essential for good health and do not provide enough energy when eaten alone.

7. Vegetables Are Good. Eat Them A Lot

Vegetables are good for you. They could be fried, boiled. It does not matter because they are healthy no matter how you prepare them.

8. Use the Olive Oil

The key to this diet is olive oil, which has been shown to lower bad cholesterol levels and increase good cholesterol levels in the body.

9. Eat Fruit for Dessert Every Day. Sometimes, Eat Cakes and Sweets Too

Eat as much fruit as you want. Always start your meal with fruits because they are low in calories and sugar levels but high in fiber.

10. Drink Lots of Water. If You Want, Drink A Little Wine Too

Drinking plenty of water can help with your digestion. And if you want, a glass of wine now and then will not do any harm. But don't go crazy with the wine. The rich antioxidants present in the wine are proven to be the best agents when it comes to fighting and protecting compromised immunity.

Food Pyramid: What It Is and How to Use It

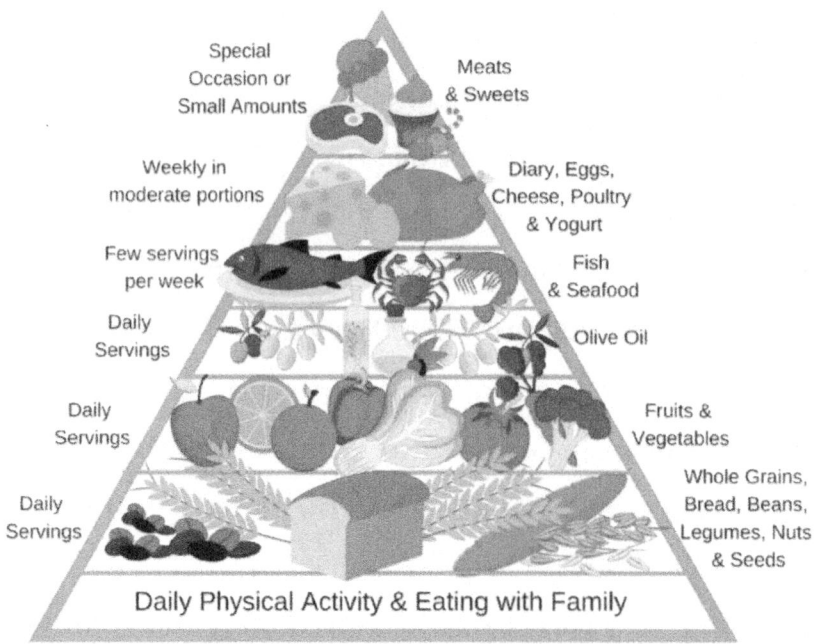

A visual representation of the Mediterranean diet, the pyramid of the Mediterranean diet provides a description of the diet, recommends a pattern of eating, and details the frequency with which particular foods ought to be eaten. This makes it possible for you to develop good eating habits and prevents you from stuffing oneself with food that is high in calories.

The Mediterranean Diet's food pyramid is substantially different from what most Americans eat on a daily basis. Meats, processed bread, grains, sugar, and trans fats are all prevalent in the American diet.

The Mediterranean Diet is essentially a mirror image of the traditional "food pyramid."

It is clear from the pyramid that the Mediterranean diet's basis is made up of legumes, whole grains, and nuts, as well as fruits and vegetables. The image is separated in this case to indicate how frequently each meal group is consumed.

Olive oil and dairy products like cheese, yogurt, and milk, in addition to cereals, nuts, legumes, fruits, and vegetables, make up a large portion of the daily diet. As a result, the Mediterranean diet is high in good fats, fiber, protein, vitamins, and minerals.

Fish, poultry, eggs, and sweets are traditionally consumed once or twice weekly in Mediterranean countries, but feel free to incorporate them into your regular diet. Simply follow our recommendations for selecting the greatest of these delectable delicacies. Pork, beef, and lamb are rare and are consumed only once or twice a month. It is also a good idea for you to keep them to once or twice a month. Saturated fats are found in animal products and should be avoided.

After some meals, a glass of red wine is enjoyed, but it is rarely overindulged. If you don't like wine or don't drink it, pure grape juice from red or Concord grapes is a great substitute, as it includes many of the same micronutrients as red wine.

Water is the preferred beverage, and a large amount of it is consumed on a daily basis.

Mediterranean Diet Health Benefits

The Mediterranean diet has been more popular in recent years, and it's easy to see why: it offers a wide variety of health benefits, from improved heart health and reduced risk of cancer to increased energy and the desire to exercise.

The scientifically-proven health benefits of the Mediterranean diet are only part of the reason for its widespread acceptance as one of the best eating plans. The diet's flexibility, emphasis on flavor and food diversity, and inclusion of items from all food groups help dispel the restrictive sensations that can accompany other eating plans.

Of course, any diet has downsides, but the Mediterranean diet may result in long-term behavioral changes and an adjustment in lifestyle, both of which are beneficial to long-term health. Here's a list of all the health benefits of eating a Mediterranean-style diet.

Lower your Chance of the Heart Diseases

If the Mediterranean diet is famous for anything, it is for being heart-healthy. As a result, it is consistently ranked as one of the top diets in the Best Diet category by the U.S.A News and the World Report.

It's easy to see why: a slew of scientific evidence suggests that a Mediterranean diet is excellent for the heart.

According to a 2016 study of over 20,000 individuals, everyone who follows the Mediterranean diet has a decreased risk of developing heart disease, and the researchers think that 4% of all cardiovascular disease cases may be avoided if everybody followed the Mediterranean diet.

Another study examined the chance of heart attacks, strokes, and cardiovascular disease mortality in persons who ate the Mediterranean diet vs. those who didn't. The five-year study discovered that persons who ate a Mediterranean diet had a 30% decreased risk of heart disease.

Possibility of Delay in Cognitive Decline

According to some research, a Mediterranean diet can help delay cognitive decline and avoid degenerative diseases like Alzheimer's disease. Further research is required, but the preliminary findings are encouraging!

A review published in Nutrition Frontiers in 2016 looked at 12 studies on diet and brain health and concluded that "there is also promising evidence that a greater connection to the Mediterranean diet is correlated with improving memory, slowing cognitive decline, or decreasing the conversion of Alzheimer's disease."

The effect of a MIND diet, which is a blend of Mediterranean and DASH diets, on the brain was investigated in a 2015 report. This diet "significantly inhibits cognitive decline," according to scientists.

While early research on the Mediterranean diet and diseases such as Alzheimer's disease cannot be utilized to reach any conclusions, it seems that some experts feel the Eating Plan and variants on it (such as the MIND diet) may help brain health.

Weight Loss Assistance

The Mediterranean diet is a good way to lose weight. A Mediterranean diet actually has been found in studies to aid with losing fat. Mediterranean diet followers lose fat at a similar pace to low-carb followers. A big study released in 2018 found that eating a Mediterranean diet lowers the risk of abdominal obesity (with over 32,000 participants).

Reduces the Chance of Having the stroke

In the same study that indicated a Mediterranean diet may prevent up to 6% of instances of heart disease, researchers discovered that it can also prevent up to 8.5% of strokes.

In addition, the 2018 study from the United Kingdom discovered that eating a Mediterranean diet decreased the chance of stroke.

Despite the fact that the study's authors emphasize that this conclusion only relates to women and that further research is needed, they do mention that additional research is required.

While research findings may be valid in one location and not in another, the association between a Mediterranean diet and a lower risk of stroke appears to exist in several areas: For nearly four years, a study released in the Council of Europe Heart Journal in the year 2016 monitored approximately 15,000 patients in around 39 countries. Individuals who followed the Mediterranean diet closely had a decreased heart attack risk, stroke, and death from heart disease.

Assist in the Reduction of Type 2 Diabetes Risk

According to one research, eating a Mediterranean diet may help you control your diabetes risk and blood sugar levels.

If you have diabetes, an expert will advise you on how to control your levels of blood sugar by following a Mediterranean diet.

Patients with Arthritis May Benefit from the Mediterranean Diet

According to limited data, the Mediterranean diet may assist persons with arthritis in lessening pain. A Mediterranean diet includes several anti-inflammatory foods, which makes sense considering that arthritis is an inflammatory disorder.

In addition, the (NIH) National Institute of Health advises omega-three fatty acids to reduce inflammation, and a Mediterranean diet provides a variety of these beneficial fats.

A 2018 systematic review of the Mediterranean diet for osteoarthritis, a degenerative form of arthritis, found that, although more long-term research is needed, the Mediterranean diet seems to reduce arthritic symptoms.

Some Cancers Might Be Protected

The Mediterranean diet is famous for protecting against chronic diseases such as diabetes, heart disease, and metabolic disease.

According to the study, this anti-inflammatory and antioxidant-rich diet helps protect against cancer.

Breast cancer, prostate cancer, liver cancer, stomach cancer, and neck and head cancer could all be prevented by following a Mediterranean diet, according to a 2017 study.

The study claims that "consuming a lot of fruits, whole grains, and vegetables are principally responsible for the favorable effect."

Possibility of Lowering LDL Cholesterol and Blood Pressure

LDL cholesterol and blood pressure (sometimes known as "negative" cholesterol) are two of the most significant risk factors for illness and health. Any exceptionally big marker may signal or be a source of health concern in and of itself.

The Mediterranean diet, for example, is one of many methods for managing and lowering blood pressure and LDL cholesterol. In 2014, scientists analyzed the diets of over 800 firefighters to see whether their eating habits impacted those health markers. They discovered that the more closely the guys followed a Mediterranean diet, the higher their cholesterol levels were.

Individualized Dietary Requirements Are Possible

The Mediterranean diet will keep you alive whether you're a vegan, paleo, vegetarian, dairy-free, gluten-free, or anything else. Obviously, the diet is most effective when every one of the foods it encourages is permitted, but you actually can tailor it to your unique needs.

The Mediterranean diet is considered non-restrictive by most experts since it has a good mix of carbs, healthy fats, proteins, vegetables, fruits, and even a few indulgences (calling all red wine fans!).

Physical Activity is Encouraged

One of the fewer diets that promote physical activities as a foundation of a healthy lifestyle is the Mediterranean diet. Most individuals in the United States do not get enough exercise, so this is a welcome improvement.

Daily exercises are also much more probably to create healthy eating choices during the day.

Yet, it is worth mentioning that the Mediterranean diet with exercise may be mutually beneficial: in a related study, researchers observed that eating a Mediterranean diet rather than a conventional Western diet might actually boost physical performance.

The Importance of Variety and Moderation is Emphasized

The Mediterranean diet may help you lose weight in the long term since it offers a broad range of foods and tastes. You will not grow fatigued or constrained. If you're prone to yo-yo dieting due to constrained emotions, the Mediterranean diet enables you to enjoy heavy carbohydrate foods, rich spices, and even wine and chocolate.

Additionally, since the Mediterranean diet emphasizes fiber-rich and protein-dense meals, hunger should be avoided even if you're on a calorie-restricted diet.

Cheese, almonds, nutritious grains, and salmon, for example, keep you fuller for longer. You'll also be prepared with healthy fats like olive oil, which will keep you satisfied for a longer period of time.

Dietary choices must be based primarily on your own values, current health condition, beliefs, lifestyle, difficulties, health goals, and dietary requirements.

While a Mediterranean diet has a slew of health benefits, it may not be the best diet for everybody, and that's fine. However, it can't hurt to give it a shot!

FAQ

Can I lose weight on this diet?

Yes! Low-fat and low-carbohydrate diets may result in similar or higher weight loss than the Mediterranean diet. This diet has also been linked to lower body fat and is the best diet for weight loss, according to studies. You can eat this way for the rest of your life, and you'll be protected from a variety of chronic diseases and ailments. With that stated, there are a few basic diet guidelines to remember that can help you lose weight: eating your main meal earlier in the day, eating largely vegetables, avoiding processed foods (especially carbohydrates), and drinking mostly water and herbal beverages.

How do I reduce meat intake?

Don't worry if you're used to eating meat virtually every day. You'll still eat meat, but it'll be prepared differently and in lower quantities.

Can a vegan follow this diet?

You can. A little-known fact about the Mediterranean diet is that, owing to religious practices, the traditional Greek diet used as a model for the Mediterranean diet was vegan for almost half of the year. Meat is only a minor component of the diet. As a result, the cuisine includes many vegan options, such as substantial vegetable meals and a variety of bean recipes such as casseroles, vegetable patties, and dips, making it an appropriate eating pattern for vegans. Grains, nuts (especially walnuts), seeds, and nut butter are other good options for vegans.

Are there gluten-free options?

Absolutely. Because the majority of the recipes are vegetable-based, people who are gluten-free have several options. Most Mediterranean meals are gluten-free, with the exception of some pasta dishes and savory pies.

Furthermore, studies have shown that people with celiac disease who previously maintained a gluten-free diet can improve their nutritional health without gaining weight by transitioning to the Mediterranean diet.

I'm diabetic. Should I follow a Mediterranean diet?

You absolutely should. While it is better renowned for its heart-health benefits, the Mediterranean diet is also beneficial to diabetics.

Studies have shown that the Mediterranean diet is associated with weight loss, reduced blood sugar, and a delayed requirement for diabetes medications compared to other diets. It's a low- to moderate-carb diet that's high in vegetables, healthy fats, and whole grains. All of these things can help to keep blood sugar levels stable. Also, it's rich in antioxidants and can play an important role in the prevention and management of diabetes.

Do I have to drink alcohol?

No. There's no reason to start drinking now if you don't already. If you drink, be aware that consuming modest to moderate amounts of red wine with food has been linked to a number of health advantages and is a staple of the Mediterranean diet. If you don't drink, you'll still reap the same incredible benefits from this diet without it.

Is this diet for the whole family?

Yes, It is. Children who eat a Mediterranean diet are more likely to maintain a healthy weight, according to research. Pregnant ladies are in the same boat. Vegetables prepared in the classic Mediterranean diet style are incredibly tasty and appealing.

What to Eat and What to Avoid

Foods to Eat

The traditional Western diet is very low in fresh fruits and vegetables and very high in starchy foods and red meat. In contrast, the Mediterranean diet is based largely on fresh produce, with whole grains at most meals, seafood several times per week, and meat only a few times per month, usually in small portions. Here is what your typical daily diet should look like:

- **Fresh fruits and vegetables: Unlimited, but at least 4 servings per day-** All fruits and vegetables are allowed on the Mediterranean diet and in unlimited quantities. The only exceptions are corn and white potatoes, which should be eaten in very limited amounts, as they are very starchy.

    Eating your fruits and vegetables raw is great, but steamed, roasted, sautéed, poached, grilled, and baked fruits and vegetables are all welcome on the Mediterranean diet. Avoid boiling vegetables, as many of the nutrients are lost in the water and the result is far less flavorful and colorful than with other cooking methods. Instead of butter and excessive salt, use olive oil and herbs in the preparation.

- **Whole grains: 3 to 5 servings per day-** Whole grains are an integral part of the Mediterranean diet and part of the reason that the diet is so rich in heart-healthful fiber. Forgo white bread and overly processed grain products and focus on whole grains such as whole wheat, oats, barley, and brown rice. Whole-grain pasta is perfectly fine, but portion sizes are much smaller in the Mediterranean than they are in the United States. Heaping plates of pasta aren't common in Italy; rather, pasta is used as a backdrop for a flavorful sauce and plenty of vegetables.

- **Healthful fats: 4 to 6 servings per day-** Healthful fats are an essential part of the Mediterranean diet. Olive oil, olives, avocados, fresh seafood and shellfish, nuts, and seeds are high in them.

- **Fish and seafood: At least 3 servings per week-** There's a reason that seafood gets an important spot on the Mediterranean Diet pyramid: eating seafood two to three times per week reduces the risk of death from any health-related cause, according to a 2006 study in the Journal of the American Medical Association.

- **Dairy products: Up to 7 servings per week-** Milk, yogurt, and cheese are welcome on the Mediterranean diet, but they are not eaten in the high quantities common in the Western diet. Choose low-fat cheeses and milk and opt for Greek yogurt whenever possible, as it contains twice the protein of regular yogurt. Generally, milk is reserved for cereal, coffee or tea, and baking. Cheese is used as a dessert or as a flavoring for soups, salads, and entrées, and cheese sauces are not a regular part of the Mediterranean diet.

- **Red wine: Up to one 5-oz. glass per day for women, two glasses per day for men-** Red wine is an important part of the Mediterranean diet and is typically enjoyed with the afternoon or evening meal, rather than on its own. The antioxidants in red wine, particularly resveratrol, are credited with improved heart health and slowed cellular aging. If you don't care for wine, try to get in several servings of red or purple fruits per week, such as grapes, raspberries, blackberries, and plums.

- **Eggs: 3 to 5 servings (of two eggs each) per week-** Eggs are traditionally enjoyed frequently in the Mediterranean diet, especially by those families that raise their own chickens. Opt for organic, free-range, hormone-free eggs. They're safer and contain more omega-3 fats than commercial eggs. Use them for baking, in sauces, and as entrées.

- **Poultry: 2 to 5 servings per week-** Poultry is eaten far more often in the Mediterranean than red meat. You can eat any cuts of chicken and turkey, although it's recommended that you remove the skin and any visible fat before eating. Game birds are also welcome on the diet, so you can choose quail, duck, pheasant, pigeon, or any other bird that you like.
- **Sweets: Up to 4 servings per week-** Although the people of the Mediterranean enjoy sweets, dessert is typically cheese and/or fruit, not sugary pastries. Go for fruit most of the week and reserve sweeter desserts for special meals with guests or as an occasional treat. Artificial sweeteners are not recommended; instead, stick with sugar, honey, and molasses in small quantities.
- **Red meat: 3 to 5 servings per month-** Red meats such as beef, pork, and lamb are generally reserved for a few special meals, and portions are much smaller than on most Western plates. Choose organic, grass-fed meats whenever possible (as they are higher in omega-3s), and leaner cuts such as sirloin or loin should be given preference over the fattier ones, such as bacon or ribs. A 3to 5-ounce steak is plenty for one meal, as opposed to a gigantic rib eye. You can also stretch your portions by using red meat as part of a hearty stew or as an ingredient in salads and soups.

Foods to Avoid

When following a Mediterranean diet, it's important to avoid foods and substances that have been processed or refined:

- **Added sugar:** Many foods have added sugar, but soda, candy, ice cream, table sugar, syrup, and baked products contain the most.
- **Refined grains:** Tortillas, chips, crackers, white bread, pasta,
- **Trans fats:** Fried foods, margarine, and other processed foods
- **Refined oils:** soybean oil, cottonseed oil, grapeseed oil, canola oil,
- **Processed meat:** Deli meats, processed sausages, hot dogs, beef jerky
- **Highly processed foods:** Microwave popcorn, fast food, convenience meals, granola bars

CHAPTER 1
BREAKFAST

1. Breakfast Quinoa Muffins	17
2. Cinnamon Apple and Lentils Porridge	17
3. Fruity Breakfast Couscous	17
4. Mediterranean Breakfast Panini	17
5. Breakfast Yogurt Quinoa	18
6. Fruity Yogurt-Topped Avocado Salad	18
7. Herb-Encrusted Italian Omelet	18
8. Harissa Shakshuka with Bell Peppers and Tomatoes	19
9. Fig and Ricotta Toast with Walnuts and Honey	20
10. Egg in a "Pepper Hole" with Avocado	20
11. Sun-Dried Tomatoes Oatmeal	20
12. Banana Choco Breakfast Smoothie	21
13. Leeks and Eggs Muffins	21
14. Apple Quinoa Breakfast Bars	21
15. Spanish Toasted Tomato Baguettes	22

1. Breakfast Quinoa Muffins

Preparation time: ten mins

Cooking time: thirty mins

Servings: twelve muffins

Ingredients:

- 3 eggs, whisked
- half sliced yellow onion
- half cup quinoa, cooked
- half cup aggravated Swiss cheese
- half cup sliced white mushrooms
- quarter cup sliced sun-dried tomatoes
- Salt & black pepper, as required

Directions:

1. Combine the entire fixings in your container.
2. Separate this mixture into a silicone muffin pot and bake in your oven at 350 deg. F for thirty mins. Serve and enjoy!

Per servings: Calories: 123kcal; Fat: 6g; Carbs: 10g; Protein: 8g

2. Cinnamon Apple and Lentils Porridge

Preparation time: 5 minutes

Cooking time: 10 minutes

Servings: 4

Ingredients:

- ½ cup walnuts, chopped
- 2 green apples, cored, peeled, and cubed
- 3 tbsp maple syrup
- 3 cups almond milk
- ½ cup red lentils
- ½ tsp cinnamon powder
- ½ cup cranberries, dried
- one teaspoon vanilla extract

Directions:

1. Heat the milk inside a pot across moderate flame. Add the walnuts, apples, maple syrup, and remaining ingredients.
2. Mix thoroughly and boil for 10 mins until fully cooked. Divide into bowls and serve.

Per servings: Calories: 150kcal; Fat: 2g; Carbs: 46g; Protein: 5g

3. Fruity Breakfast Couscous

Preparation time: ten mins

Cooking time: 5 mins

Servings: four

Ingredients:

- one cinnamon stick
- 3 cups almond milk
- one-quarter tsp Himalayan salt
- 2 tbsp raw honey (extra for serving)
- 1/4 cup dried raisins
- 1/2 cup dried apricots, chopped
- 1 cup raw whole-wheat couscous
- 4 tsp melted butter

Directions:

1. Add the milk and cinnamon to a pot and let it simmer, but do not boil. Remove it from the flame.
2. Include the couscous, apricots, raisins, honey, and salt then mix it well. Cover the pot and set aside for 15 minutes. Drizzle it with butter and serve.

Per servings: Calories: 333kcal; Fat: 8g; Carbs: 54g; Protein: 12g

4. Mediterranean Breakfast Panini

Preparation time: 10 minutes

Cooking time: 0 minutes

Servings: 4

Ingredients:

- 1 (12 oz.) round panini loaf
- two tbsps. additional-virgin olive oil
- 8 large eggs, hard-boiled & sliced into rounds
- 1/2 cup black olives, pitted & halved
- 2 heirloom tomatoes, thinly sliced into rounds
- 12 large, fresh basil leaves

Directions:

1. Cut the panini loaf in half horizontally and use a basting brush to coat the interior of each half with 1 tbsp of olive oil.

2. Arrange the panini with all the ingredients. Slice and serve.

Per servings: Calories: 427kcal; Fat: 21g; Carbs: 39g; Protein: 23g

5. Breakfast Yogurt Quinoa

Preparation time: five mins
Cooking time: 10 mins
Servings: 2
Ingredients:

- 1 cinnamon stick
- one inch knob of ginger, peeled
- half cup quinoa
- 3/4 cups water
- 1/2 cup plain Greek yogurt
- 1/4 cup chopped almonds
- 1/4 cup pitted & chopped dates
- kosher salt to taste

Directions:

1. Boil the water, quinoa, cinnamon sticks, ginger, and salt inside your medium pot across high flame.

2. Adjust to a low boil, covered for ten-twelve mins. Eliminate the cinnamon sticks and ginger. Fluff the quinoa with a fork.

3. Add the yogurt, dates, and almonds to the quinoa then mix it well. Divide evenly among 4 bowls and serve.

Per servings: Calories: 280kcal; Fat: 11g; Carbs: 37g; Protein: 13g

6. Fruity Yogurt-Topped Avocado Salad

Preparation time: ten mins
Cooking time: zero mins
Servings: 6
Ingredients:

- 3 medium ripe avocados, skinned and diced
- 2 tbsp lemon juice, +1 tsp if needed
- 1 tsp finely grated lemon zest
- 1 tbsp raw honey
- half cup plain Greek yogurt
- one medium-sized firm banana, sliced
- 11 oz canned mandarin oranges, drained
- 1 cup seedless grapes
- 1 granny smith apple, chopped

Directions:

1. Cover the avocados with lemon juice inside a large container.

2. Whisk the yogurt, honey, lemon zest, and remaining lemon juice in another container.

3. Include the apple, grapes, oranges, and banana to the bowl with the avocado. Mix it well.

4. Serve with yogurt mixture on top.

Per servings: Calories: 231kcal; Fat: 11g; Carbs: 35g; Protein: 3g

7. Herb-Encrusted Italian Omelet

Preparation time: 10 mins
Cooking time: fifteen mins
Servings: 4
Ingredients:

- 1 tablespoon extra-virgin olive oil
- quarter cup shallots, thinly sliced
- one large Yukon gold potato, thinly sliced
- 1/8 tsp white pepper
- 1/8 tsp cayenne pepper
- 1/4 tsp Himalayan salt
- 1/4 tsp dried thyme, crushed
- 1/4 tsp dried rosemary, crushed
- 6 large free-range eggs
- 2 tbsp grated mozzarella cheese

Directions:

1. Place the wire rack in the center of the oven and set the oven broiler to preheat on high.

2. Cook the shallots for 3 minutes in a pan. Remove the shallots. Place the sliced potatoes in one layer at the bottom of the pan.

3. Set the oven broiler to preheat on high, with the wire rack in the center of the oven.

4. Include the pepper, cayenne pepper, salt, thyme, rosemary, and eggs to the bowl of shallots. Lightly whisk until the eggs are light and fluffy.

5. Place the egg solution across the potatoes. Conceal the pan with foil. Bake in the oven for 4-6 minutes. Remove the pan from the oven then discard the foil.

6. Sprinkle the cheese over the omelet before returning the pot to the microwave and broiling for two to five mins till lightly toasted.

7. Allow the omelet to rest for about 5 minutes outside the oven before slicing and serving.

Per servings: Calories: 204kcal; Fat: 12g; Carbs: 13g; Protein: 11g

8. Harissa Shakshuka with Bell Peppers and Tomatoes

Preparation time: ten mins

Cooking time: twenty mins

Servings: 4

Ingredients:

- one and a half tbsp extra-virgin olive oil
- two tbsp harissa
- one tbsp tomato paste
- ½ onion, diced
- one bell pepper, seeded & diced
- 3 garlic cloves, crushed
- one (twenty-eight oz) can of no-salt-included diced tomatoes
- ½ tsp kosher salt
- 4 large eggs
- 2 to 3 tbsp fresh basil, chopped or cut into ribbons

Directions:

1. Warm the microwave to 375 deg. F.

2. Add the olive oil to your ovenproof griddle across moderate flame. Sauté the onion, bell pepper, harissa, and tomato paste 3 to 4 minutes.

3. Include the garlic and cook thirty secs till perfumed. Include the diced tomatoes and salt and simmer for 10 mins.

4. Establish four holes in the sauce surface and add one egg to every. Transfer to the microwave and bake for 10-12 mins till the whites are cooked and the yolks are set.

5. Allow to cool for 3 to 5 minutes, garnish with the basil, and carefully spoon onto plates.

Per servings: Calories: 190kcal; Fat: 10g; Carbs: 15g; Protein: 9g

9. Fig and Ricotta Toast with Walnuts and Honey

Preparation time: five mins

Cooking time: 0 mins

Servings: two

Ingredients:

- ¼ cup ricotta cheese
- 2 whole-wheat bread, toasted
- 4 figs, halved
- 2 tbsp walnuts, chopped
- 1 tsp honey

Directions:

1. Spread 2 tablespoons of ricotta cheese on each piece of toast. Add 4 fig halves to each piece of toast, pressing firmly to keep the figs in the ricotta.

2. Sprinkle 1 tablespoon of walnuts and drizzle ½ teaspoon of honey on each piece of toast.

Per servings: Calories: 215kcal; Fat: 10g; Carbs: 26g; Protein: 7g

10. Egg in a "Pepper Hole" with Avocado

Preparation time: 15 minutes

Cooking time: 4-5 minutes

Servings: 4

Ingredients:

- 4 bell peppers, any color
- 1 tbsp extra-virgin olive oil
- 8 large eggs
- ¾ tsp kosher salt, divided
- ¼ tsp freshly ground black pepper, divided
- 1 avocado, peeled, pitted, & diced
- ¼ cup red onion, diced
- ¼ cup fresh basil, chopped
- Juice of ½ lime

Directions:

1. Stem and seed the bell peppers. Cut 2 (2-inch-thick) rings from each pepper. Chop the remaining bell pepper into small pieces and cast away.

2. Warm the oil in your big griddle across moderate flame.

3. Include 4 bell pepper rings then crack 1 egg in the middle of each ring—season with ¼ tsp salt and ⅛ tsp black pepper then cook within two-three mins.

4. Gently toss and cook 1 additional minute for over-easy.

5. Move the egg–bell pepper rings to a platter or onto plates and repeat with the remaining 4 bell pepper rings.

6. In a medium bowl, combine the avocado, onion, basil, lime juice, reserved diced bell pepper, the remaining salt, and black pepper. Divide among the 4 plates and serve.

Per servings: Calories: 270kcal; Fat: 19g; Carbs: 12g; Protein: 15g

11. Sun-Dried Tomatoes Oatmeal

Preparation time: 15 minutes

Cooking time: 25 minutes

Servings: 2

Ingredients:

- 1 1/2 cup water
- 1/2 cup almond milk
- 1/2 cup steel-cut oats
- 1/8 cup sun-dried tomatoes, sliced
- one tablespoon olive oil
- red pepper flakes, as required

Directions:

1. Combine the water with the milk in a skillet and let it boil across moderate flame.

2. In the meantime, warm the oil in your pan across moderate-high flame. Include the oats and cook 2 minutes. Transfer this mixture to the skillet with the milk mixture.

3. Stir well, include the tomatoes, and low boil 23 minutes across moderate flame.

4. Divide it into containers, drizzle the red pepper flakes on surface, and distribute.

Per servings: Calories: 170kcal; Fat: 17g; Carbs: 16g; Protein: 2g

12. Banana Choco Breakfast Smoothie

Preparation time: 10 minutes
Cooking time: 0 minutes
Servings: 2
Ingredients:
- 1 large frozen banana, peeled
- 1 1/4 cup almond milk
- 1/2 cup frozen blueberries
- 2 tbsp chia seeds
- 2 tbsp unsweetened cocoa powder
- 2 tbsp almond butter

Directions:
1. Inside a mixer, add the entire components.
2. Mix to combine until uniform and serve.

Per servings: Calories: 300kcal; Fat: 16g; Carbs: 37g; Protein: 8g

13. Leeks and Eggs Muffins

Preparation time: 10 minutes
Cooking time: 20 minutes
Servings: 2
Ingredients:
- 3 eggs, whisked
- ¼ cup baby spinach
- 2 tbsp leeks, chopped
- 4 tbsp parmesan, grated
- 2 tbsp almond milk
- 1 small red bell pepper, sliced
- one tomato, cubed
- two tbsps. cheddar cheese, grated
- Salt & black pepper, as required
- Cooking spray

Directions:
1. Combine the eggs with the milk, salt, pepper, and remaining components, excluding for the cooking spray, inside a container.

2. Oil a muffin tin with the cooking spray and divide the egg solution in every muffin mold. Bake in the oven at 380 deg. F for 20 minutes and serve for breakfast.

Per servings: Calories: 308kcal; Fat: 19g; Carbs: 8g; Protein: 24g

14. Apple Quinoa Breakfast Bars

Preparation time: fifteen mins
Cooking time: 40 mins
Servings: 12
Ingredients:
- 2 eggs
- one apple peeled and sliced into ½-inch chunks
- one cup unsweetened apple sauce
- one and a half cups cooked & cooled quinoa
- 1½ cups rolled oats
- ¼ cup peanut butter
- 1 tsp vanilla
- ½ tsp cinnamon
- ¼ cup coconut oil
- ½ tsp baking powder

Directions:
1. Warm your microwave to 350 deg. F, oil your 8x8 inch baking dish using oil, and set it aside.

2. Stir the apple sauce, cinnamon, coconut oil, peanut butter, vanilla, and eggs in a large bowl.

3. Add the cooked quinoa, rolled oats, and baking powder then mix till entirely merged. Include the apples and gently fold in the mixture.

4. Place this solution into your baking dish, bake for 40 mins, and let it cool before slicing.

Per servings: Calories: 230kcal; Fat: 10g; Carbs: 31g; Protein: 7g

15. Spanish Toasted Tomato Baguettes

Preparation time: 10 minutes
Cooking time: 8 minutes
Servings: 4
Ingredients:

- 2 baguettes, halved lengthwise
- 4 tsp crushed garlic
- 2 ripe heirloom tomatoes, grated
- 2 tbsp extra-virgin olive oil
- 4 thin slices of smoked ham
- Freshly ground black pepper, as required
- 1 teaspoon flaky sea salt

Directions:

1. Preheat your oven to 500 degrees Fahrenheit and place a wire rack in the center. Toast the baguette halves 6 to 8 minutes until crispy.

2. Spread 1 tsp of crushed garlic over the face of each baguette. Top the garlic with a tomato.

3. Sprinkle each baguette with oil and top each with a slice of ham—season with salt and pepper to taste.

Per servings: Calories: 267kcal; Fat: 15g; Carbs: 15g; Protein: 18g

CHAPTER 2
BEANS, RICE & GRAINS

16. Basil And Sun-Dried Tomatoes Rice	24
17. Sprouts Of Alfalfa And Hummus	24
18. Bean And Cabbage Soup	24
19. Cucumber Olive Rice	25
20. Sweet Rice Pudding	25
21. Rice And Veggie Jambalaya	26
22. Baked Mediterranean Rice	26
23. Zucchini With Rice And Tzatziki	27
24. Radicchio And Smoked Bacon Risotto	27
25. Mediterranean Spiced Lentils	28
26. Spanish Rice Casserole With Cheesy Beef	28
27. Herbed Rice	29
28. Savory Greek White Fava Beans	29
29. Baked Black-Eyed Peas	30
30. Lemon Mushroom Rice	30

16. Basil And Sun-Dried Tomatoes Rice

Preparation time: ten mins

Cooking time: twenty-five mins

Servings: four

Ingredients:

- 5 cups chicken stock
- one yellow onion, chopped
- 1 (10 oz) can of sun-dried tomatoes in olive oil, drained & chopped
- 2 cups Arborio rice
- Salt & black pepper, as required
- one and a half cup parmesan, grated
- two tbsps. olive oil
- ¼ cup basil leaves, chopped

Directions:

1. Warm up a pot via the oil across moderate flame and sauté the onion and tomatoes five mins.
2. Include the rice, stock, and remaining components, except for the parmesan. Let it simmer and cook across moderate flame for twenty mins.
3. Add the parmesan, whisk, split the mix among plates, and distribute.

Per servings: Calories: 426kcal; Fat: 8g; Carbs: 56g; Protein: 7g

17. Sprouts Of Alfalfa And Hummus

Preparation time: fifteen mins

Cooking time: zero mins

Servings: 12

Ingredients:

- Twelve whole grain crackers, 12 oz.
- 1/2 quarts hummus
- 12 low-fat cheddar cheese slices
- 12 tablespoons sprouted alfalfa
- pepper, freshly ground
- Garnish with lemon wedges

Directions:

1. Place crackers on a serving plate.
2. On top of the crackers, evenly distribute the hummus.
3. Add a piece of cheddar cheese, sprout, and a pinch of pepper to each cracker.
4. Before serving, garnish the plate with lime wedges to drizzle over the crackers.

Per servings: Calories: 560kcal; Fat: 0g; Carbs: 1g; Protein: 1g

18. Bean And Cabbage Soup

Preparation time: ten mins

Cooking time: 50 mins

Servings: 6

Ingredients:

- ¼ cup olive oil
- ½ cup sliced onion
- two celery stalks, chopped
- two carrots, sliced
- 14.5-ounce can have diced tomatoes
- ¼ tsp. dried sage
- 6 sprigs parsley
- One bay leaf
- 8 cups water (14.5-ounce) tin of cannellini beans, drained
- ½ pound baked ham, diced
- 6 cups chopped green cabbage
- ½ pound Yukon potatoes, diced
- ¼ cup instant polenta
- Sea salt
- Black pepper

Directions:

1. Warm up extra virgin olive oil until hot inside a big stockpot set across moderate flame; stir in the

onions, celery, carrots, and fry for almost seven mins or until the onions are translucent.

2. Incorporate tomatoes, sage, parsley, and bay leaf; heat to low then low boil for 10 mins or so.

3. Stir in water over medium-high heat, bringing towards a rolling boil.

4. Mix in the beans, ham, potatoes, and cabbage, and diminish the flame to moderate-low.

5. Cook 'til the potatoes are soft, or about 20 minutes.

6. Mix in the polenta; boil and top alongside sea salt and pepper for around 5 mins.

7. Put the soup into containers and immediately distribute.

Per servings: Calories: 84kcal; Fat: 0.3g; Carbs: 16.4g; Protein: 4.3g

19. Cucumber Olive Rice

Preparation time: 55 mins

Cooking time: 15 mins

Servings: eight

Ingredients:

- 1 cup of parsley leaves
- three garlic cloves
- Black pepper, as required
- 3 sliced cucumbers
- 1 cup mint leaves
- 1 lb. of heirloom
- Kosher salt to taste
- 1 cup of feta
- 1 chopped onion
- 7 tablespoons olive oil
- one and a half cups of brown rice
- three tbsps. sherry vinegar

Directions:

1. Inside a hot frying pan, add two tablespoons of oil.

2. After that, include the garlic and salt and boil for another five mins. While stirring, cook till the mixture is fragrant and translucent. Place this inside a mixing dish.

3. Reheat the frying pan & add one tablespoon of oil and the rice. Cook for 3 mins, constantly mixing, until brown and nutty.

4. Fill the dish halfway with water, then bring it to a boil. Only mix it once, then reduce the flame to a low setting and conceal it. Cook until the rice is tender and the water has been absorbed. Eliminate it from the flame and set it aside to cool for around 5 mins.

5. Place the rice inside a container using the onion mixture and set aside to cool for around 20 mins.

6. Combine vinegar, cucumbers, tomatoes, and the rest of the oil in a mixing bowl—season using black pepper and sea salt.

7. Finally, Serve with cheese, parsley, and mint on top.

Per servings: Calories: 223kcal; Fat: 13g; Carbs: 24g; Protein: 5g

20. Sweet Rice Pudding

Preparation time: ten mins

Cooking time: thirty mins

Servings: 4

Ingredients:

- ¼ cup dark chocolate, chopped
- one teaspoon liquid stevia
- 1 ¼ cup rice
- one-third cup coconut butter
- two and a half cups almond milk
- 1 tsp. vanilla

Directions:

1. Inside the saucepan, combine all ingredients & stir well. Cook for around 20 minutes on high, covered.

Allow for natural pressure release after you've finished. Take off the cover. Serve with a good stir.

Per servings: Calories: 638kcal; Fat: 40g; Carbs: 63g; Protein: 9g

21. Rice And Veggie Jambalaya

Preparation time: twenty mins

Cooking time: 55 mins

Servings: four

Ingredients:

- two tbsps. olive oil
- two celery stalks, chopped
- ½ red bell pepper, seeded and chopped
- 1 (14-ounce) can of crushed tomatoes (low-sodium)
- 4 cups low-sodium vegetable broth
- 2 tablespoons low-sodium soy sauce
- 1 teaspoon dried thyme, crushed
- 1 teaspoon dried oregano, crushed
- ½ teaspoon smoked paprika
- Salt and black pepper to taste
- 1 scallion, chopped
- 1 onion, chopped
- 4 garlic cloves, minced
- ½ green bell pepper, seeded & sliced
- 2 cups brown rice, uncooked
- 2 tablespoons Tabasco sauce
- two bay leaves
- one tsp. dried basil, minced
- one tsp. sweet paprika
- half tsp. cayenne pepper
- three cups canned low-sodium mixed beans (chickpeas, white beans, and kidney beans)

Directions:

1. In a huge pan placed over medium heat, sauté the olive oil, onion, and garlic for about 5 minutes.

2. Add the celery and bell peppers and sauté for about 5 minutes.

3. Stir in the crushed tomatoes, broth, rice, Tabasco sauce, bay leaves, soy sauce, dried herbs, spices, and black pepper, and let it boil.

4. Reduce the heat to low, cover the pan, then simmer for about 40 minutes, occasionally stirring, until the rice is cooked.

5. Uncover the lid and mix in the beans and salt.

6. Boil for about 3 mins until heated through.

7. Reduce the heat and distribute embellished with the scallions.

Per servings: Calories: 518kcal; Fat: 11.2g; Carbs: 89g; Protein: 16g

22. Baked Mediterranean Rice

Preparation time: 20 mins

Cooking time: thirty mins

Servings: eight

Ingredients:

- ½ cup sweet onion, diced
- Olive oil cooking spray
- 1½ cups arborio rice
- 2 tablespoons unsalted butter, melted
- 1 cup mozzarella cheese, shredded
- 2 tablespoons fresh basil, chopped
- 2 tablespoons fresh oregano, chopped
- 1 teaspoon salt
- ¼ cup parmesan cheese, grated
- 3 cups low-sodium chicken broth
- 1-pint cherry tomatoes, cut in half
- 8 ounces baby spinach, stem and tips removed

Directions:

1. Preheat the oven to 375 deg. F then grease a casserole dish with the olive oil cooking spray.

2. Mix the chicken broth with the oregano, basil, and salt, and cast away.

3. Arrange the rice and onions in the casserole dish and drizzle the melted butter on top.

4. Whisk to cover well and mix in the chicken broth mixture.

5. Position the tomato halves on top of the rice and bake for thirty mins.

6. Eliminate from the microwave and fold the mozzarella cheese and baby spinach into the baked rice.

7. Top with parsley and parmesan cheese.

8. Wrap with foil and leave for 5 mins, then distribute.

Per servings: Calories: 211kcal; Fat: 5.3g; Carbs: 33.1g; Protein: 7.8g

23. Zucchini With Rice And Tzatziki

Preparation time: 15 minutes

Cooking time: 35 minutes

Servings: 4

Ingredients:

- 3 zucchinis, diced
- ¼ cup of olive oil
- 1 cup of short-grain rice
- 1 chopped onion
- ½ cup of sliced fresh dill
- one cup vegetable broth
- Salt
- 2 tablespoons pine nuts
- Freshly ground black pepper
- 1 cup of Tzatziki sauce

Directions:

1. Inside a heavy-bottomed pan, warm the oil on medium flame. Mix in the onion & cook for around five mins on medium-low flame—cook for another 2 mins after adding the zucchini.

2. Season using salt & pepper after adding the vegetable broth & dill. Raise the mixture to a simmer by increasing the flame to medium.

3. Return the mixture to a boil after adding the rice. Reduce to a very low flame, cover, and simmer for around 15 minutes. Remove from the heat and set aside for 10 minutes to cool. Serve alongside tzatziki sauce and a scoop of rice on a serving dish topped with pine nuts.

Per servings: Calories: 414kcal; Fat: 17g; Carbs: 47g; Protein: 5g

24. Radicchio And Smoked Bacon Risotto

Preparation time: ten mins

Cooking time: 30 mins

Servings: 3

Ingredients:

- 3.4 fl. ounces (100ml) red wine
- 1 ½ cup rice
- Table salt to taste
- 14 oz. of radicchio
- 3 sprigs of thyme
- 5.3 oz. of smoked bacon
- Black pepper to taste
- 7 teaspoons of extra virgin olive oil
- 34 fl. oz. of Vegetable broth
- 4 tablespoons of shallots

Directions:

1. Let's get started by making the veggie broth.

2. Begin with the radicchio, which should be sliced in half and the middle portion removed (the white part). It should be cut into strips, rinsed thoroughly, and placed aside. Smoked bacon should also be cut into small-sized pieces.

3. Place the shallot with a little oil in a pan and finely chop it. Allow simmering on medium flame, adding a ladle of liquid if needed, before adding the bacon and browning it.

4. Add the rice after about 2 minutes and toast it, stirring often. Put the red wine over a high flame at this point.

5. Continue to boil after the alcohol has evaporated, adding a ladle of broth at a time. Allow the preceding one to dry completely before applying another—season with salt & black pepper to taste (how much you use is up to you).

6. Add the radicchio strips at the end of the cooking process. Mix them with the rice until fully combined, but don't cook them. Add the thyme, chopped.

Per servings: Calories: 482kcal; Fat: 17g; Carbs: 68g; Protein: 13g

25. Mediterranean Spiced Lentils

Preparation time: 5 minutes
Cooking time: 20 minutes
Servings: 6
Ingredients:

- 1 teaspoon dried oregano
- ¾ cup green lentils
- 1 teaspoon dried basil
- ¼ teaspoon ground sage
- 2¼ cups water
- ½ teaspoon dried parsley
- ¼ teaspoon onion powder

Directions:

1. Add the lentils, water, and spices in a heavy pot placed across moderate-high flame.

2. Let the ingredients boil, and then cover with a lid.

3. Diminish the flame, afterwards low boil for about 20 mins.

4. Stir well and serve hot.

Per servings: Calories: 258kcal; Fat: 0.9g; Carbs: 44.1g; Protein: 18.7g

26. Spanish Rice Casserole With Cheesy Beef

Preparation time: ten mins
Cooking time: twenty-five mins
Servings: four
Ingredients:

- 1 red bell pepper
- 16.8 oz. of Spanish Rice mix
- 2 tablespoons of crumbled queso fresco
- one-third cup of sour cream
- half cup Monterey Jack cheese
- one tablespoon olive oil
- one cup of corn
- one avocado sliced
- 1 cup of meatless crumbles
- quarter cup of salsa

Directions:

1. Rice should be cooked in a two and a half liter casserole dish that can be microwaved.

2. Warm up your oven to 375°F.

3. Put the oil in a skillet, then heat it.

4. Cook till the bell pepper is soft, around five to seven mins.

5. After the rice is done, mix the bell pepper, sour cream, cooked, meatless crumbles, salsa, and corn.

6. Lastly, drizzle the cheese on surface.

7. Bake it for around ten mins until the cheese is dissolved and browned.

8. Serve with sliced avocado on top.

Per servings: Calories: 437kcal; Fat: 22g; Carbs: 46g; Protein: 13g

27. Herbed Rice

Preparation time: 10 Mins

Cooking time: twenty Mins

Servings: four

Ingredients:

- one teaspoon salt
- two tablespoons olive oil
- one onion, chopped
- 1 teaspoon black pepper
- 3 cups chicken broth
- 1 teaspoon garlic, minced
- ¼ cup lemon juice
- ½ cup basmati rice
- ½ teaspoon each of dried rosemary, basil, dill, parsley, oregano, and thyme

Directions:

1. Melt the olive oil inside a pan on moderate flame. Include the salt and black pepper.

2. Include the onion and cook till it has tendered. Include the garlic afterwards cook for a min.

3. Include the chicken broth, lemon juice, and dried herbs and rice. Continue whisking till combined.

4. Wait for the mixture to boil, then conceal and lower the heat.

5. Continue cooking till the rice is thoroughly tendered.

6. Distribute and relish.

Per servings: Calories: 227kcal; Fat: 0g; Carbs: 49g; Protein: 4g

28. Savory Greek White Fava Beans

Preparation time: ten mins

Cooking time: 45 mins

Servings: four

Ingredients:

- one and a quarter cup white fava beans, dry
- Three sage leaves, fresh
- Season with salt to taste
- Two fresh garlic cloves, coarsely minced
- One finely chopped tiny onion
- One finely sliced celery stalk
- Three tbsp. freshly squeezed lemon juice
- half tsp. oregano, dry
- Three tbsp extra-virgin olive oil
- Red wine vinegar (4 1/2 tablespoons)
- To taste freshly ground pepper

Directions:

1. Soak the beans in fresh water overnight (enough water to cover the beans twice their capacity).

2. Drain the beans in the morning, rinse with new water, and drain again.

3. In a large pot, combine the drained beans with 1 quart of new water and bring to a boil.

4. Cook for about 45 minutes after adding the sage and covering the pot.

5. Stir gently and dress using salt as required.

6. Simmer for a further 15 minutes, or until the beans are tender but not mushy.

7. Eliminate the pan from the fire and drain.

8. Toss beans with garlic, onion, celery, lemon juice, oregano, olive oil, and vinegar when they have cooled slightly.

9. Before serving, season with pepper to taste and put in the fridge for one hr or lengthier.

Per servings: Calories: 202kcal; Fat: 13g; Carbs: 9g; Protein: 6g

29. Baked Black-Eyed Peas

Preparation time: 15 minutes

Cooking time: 35 minutes

Servings: 3

Ingredients:

- 2 (15-ounce) cans of black-eyed peas, drained & rinsed
- three tbsps. additional-virgin olive oil
- Salt, as required
- 2 teaspoons Za'atar
- 2 teaspoons sumac
- 2 teaspoons harissa

Directions:

1. Warm up the microwave to 400 deg. F.

2. Place the black-eyed peas on a baking sheet and sprinkle using olive oil.

3. Top alongside salt and toss to coat well.

4. Bake for about 35 minutes, shaking the baking pan three times during cooking.

5. Eliminate from the microwave and season with the Za'atar, sumac, and harissa.

6. Offer warmed up.

Per servings: Calories: 478kcal; Fat: 18.5g; Carbs: 66.1g; Protein: 14.9g

30. Lemon Mushroom Rice

Preparation time: ten mins

Cooking time: thirty mins

Servings: four

Ingredients:

- 2 cups chicken stock
- 1 yellow onion, chopped
- ½ pound white mushrooms, sliced
- 2 garlic cloves, minced
- 8 oz wild rice
- Juice & zest of one lemon
- one tbsp chives, sliced
- 6 tbsp goat cheese, crumbled
- Salt & black pepper, as required

Directions:

1. Warm up a pan alongside the stock across moderate flame. Include the rice, onion, and remaining ingredients, except for the chives and cheese.

2. Let it simmer and cook for 25 minutes. Add the chives and cheese and continue to cook for 5 minutes. Divide between plates and serve.

Per servings: Calories: 222kcal; Fat: 5g; Carbs: 12g; Protein: 5g

CHAPTER 3
PASTA & COUSCOUS

31. Couscous Pudding	32
32. Chicken and Bow Tie Pasta	32
33. Pesto Chicken Pasta	32
34. Veggie Spaghetti	33
35. Mango And Pasta Salad	33
36. Italian Minestrone	34
37. Spinach Pesto Pasta	34
38. Pecorino Pasta With Sausage And Tomato	35
39. Salmon And Couscous	35
40. Maccheroni With Cherry Tomatoes And Anchovies	36
41. Delicious Chicken Pasta	36
42. Pork And Herbed Couscous Mix	37
43. Confetti Couscous	37
44. Sicilian Spaghetti	37
45. Couscous And Apricots Bowls	38
46. Broccoli And Tomato Pasta	38
47. Simple Tuna Pasta	39
48. Cinnamon Couscous And Cauliflower	39
49. Turkey And Couscous	39
50. Mediterranean Farfalle	40

31. Couscous Pudding

Preparation time: 15 mins

Cooking time: 2 mins

Servings: four

Ingredients:

- one cup couscous
- two tbsps. rose water
- 2 cups fruit juice
- 3 tablespoons butter
- ¼ cup pistachio, grated
- ¼ cup almonds, blanched
- ½ cup sugar
- 1 tablespoon cinnamon powder
- ½ cup pomegranate seeds

Directions:

1. In a large saucepan, mix fruit juice with rose water and couscous, bring to a boil over medium heat, cover, take off heat, leave aside for 15 minutes and fluff with a fork.

2. Add melted butter, almonds and pistachios, stir, divide into containers, drizzle the remaining ingredients on surface and distribute.

Per servings: Calories: 200kcal; Fat: 2g; Carbs: 4g; Protein: 7g

32. Chicken and Bow Tie Pasta

Preparation time: ten mins

Cooking time: 15 mins

Servings: four

Ingredients:

- one lb. of farfalle pasta
- 4 baked chicken breasts, halved
- 1 tomato, chopped
- 1 (8 oz) bottle of Italian salad dressing

Directions:

1. Mix the cubed chicken and 2/3 cup of salad dressing in a bowl.

2. Cook the pasta according to the package guidelines.

3. Drain thoroughly and add to the chicken mixture.

4. Toss it well and add more dressing and chopped tomato.

5. Toss it again until the pasta is fully coated and serve.

Per servings: Calories: 300kcal; Fat: 8g; Carbs: 30g; Protein: 25g

33. Pesto Chicken Pasta

Preparation time: ten mins

Cooking time: 20 mins

Servings: 3

Ingredients:

- one pound of boneless chicken breast
- 2 garlic cloves
- one-third cup of basil pesto
- Black pepper
- 1/2 lb. of whole-wheat penne pasta
- 1.5 cups of chicken broth
- 1 cup of milk
- two tbsps. butter
- quarter cup grated parmesan
- quarter cup cream cheese
- A tweak of red pepper

Directions:

1. Cut the chicken breast into one inch parts using a sharp knife. Then heat the butter in a frypan.

2. Across moderate flame, cook the chicken till it begins to brown.

3. Toss in the chopped garlic—cook for one min with the garlic & chicken in the frying pan.

4. Toss in the noodles and chicken broth with the garlic and chicken.

5. Cover the frying pan and raise to a boil across high flame.

6. After the broth has thoroughly boiled, include the pasta and cook for eight mins on low flame.

7. Include cream cheese, milk, & pesto once the pasta is soft and most of the stock has been absorbed.

8. Cook, constantly stirring, till the cream cheese has completely melted.

9. Finally, stir in the chopped parmesan till everything is well blended.

1. Add the spinach and sun-dried tomatoes if using. Remove the pasta from the flame once the spinach has wilted. Serve with crushed pepper and a tweak of red pepper on top.

Per servings: Calories: 748kcal; Fat: 41g; Carbs: 52g; Protein: 41g

34. Veggie Spaghetti

Preparation time: ten mins
Cooking time: fifteen mins
Servings: four
Ingredients:

- two zucchinis cut in rounds
- 1 pound plum tomatoes cut in halves
- Salt and black pepper as required
- 2 small eggplants sliced into rounds
- one red onion, sliced
- one red bell pepper, roughly sliced
- one garlic head
- ¼ cup olive oil
- one teaspoon herbs de Provence
- ¾ cup kalamata olives, pitted and chopped
- 2 tablespoons basil, chopped
- 12 ounces spaghetti
- 2 teaspoons marjoram, chopped
- ½ cup feta cheese, crumbled

Directions:

1. In a bowl, mix tomatoes with eggplant, red pepper, zucchini, garlic and onion with herbs, salt, pepper and three tablespoons oil, toss, place them on the preheated grill, cook for 8 minutes, chop them except the garlic, transfer to a bowl, add half of the olives and toss.

2. Put garlic in a mixing bowl, include the remaining olives and the oil and blend thoroughly.

3. Put water in a saucepan, bring to a boil over medium-high heat, add salt, add spaghetti, cook according to instructions, drain and reserve ½ cup of the cooking water.

4. Mix veggies with half of the garlic sauce, basil, marjoram and pasta in a bowl, and stir and transfer everything to a pot.

5. Warm across moderate flame, include reserved cooking liquid and the rest of the garlic sauce, stir, divide between plates, sprinkle the cheese on top and serve.

Per servings: Calories: 340kcal; Fat: 23g; Carbs: 32g; Protein: 13g

35. Mango And Pasta Salad

Preparation time: ten mins
Cooking time: 6 mins
Servings: eight
Ingredients:

- two quarts water
- 12 ounces fusilli pasta
- A pinch of salt
- 1 avocado, pitted, peeled, and sliced
- one cup red bell pepper, sliced

- one small cucumber, sliced
- 2 mangos, skinned and cubed
- Some black sesame seeds
- 1/3 cup olive oil
- one garlic clove, crushed
- two tablespoons lime juice
- one teaspoon mustard
- Black pepper, as required

Directions:

1. Place the water inside a huge saucepan, raise to a boil across moderate-high flame, include pasta, cook according to instructions and drain well.

2. Within a salad container, combine pasta with avocado and the remaining components, toss to coat, and serve.

Per servings: Calories: 243kcal; Fat: 4g; Carbs: 22g; Protein: 6g

36. Italian Minestrone

Preparation time: ten mins
Cooking time: thirty mins
Servings: 6
Ingredients:

- one cup of diced yellow onion
- one tablespoon olive oil
- 1 cup of diced zucchini
- 4 cups of vegetable broth
- 1 cup of diced celery
- 1 cup of diced yellow squash
- 1 cup of whole-wheat pasta
- one tsp. of chopped dried oregano
- Black pepper, as required
- 1 tablespoon of minced garlic
- 2 cups of red beans
- 1 bay leaf
- 1 cup of diced carrots
- 2 tablespoons of tomato paste
- 3 1/2 cups of diced tomatoes
- 1 teaspoon of salt
- 2 rosemary sprigs
- two tsps. chopped parsley
- one cup green beans

Directions:

1. Sauté the onions. Inside a Dutch oven on a high flame, cook carrots & celery in heated olive oil for around 5 minutes.

2. Cook for around two more minutes after combining the squash & zucchini.

3. Cook, stirring in the garlic & tomato paste.

4. Fill the pot with vegetable stock. Toss the tomatoes, rosemary, salt, bay leaf, and oregano.

5. Allow it to come to a boil and then reduce to a low flame.

6. Cook for around ten minutes after combining pasta and red beans.

7. Cook for 3 minutes after adding the green beans.

8. By adding the stock, you can adjust the consistency.

9. Before serving, taste and adjust the seasonings.

Per servings: Calories: 278kcal; Fat: 7g; Carbs: 44g; Protein: 13g

37. Spinach Pesto Pasta

Preparation time: ten Mins
Cooking time: ten Mins
Servings: four
Ingredients:

- eight ounces of whole-grain pasta
- one-third cup mozzarella cheese, aggravated
- half cup pesto
- five ounces of fresh spinach
- one full and three-quarter cups water

- eight ounces mushrooms, sliced
- one tablespoon olive oil
- Salt and black pepper, as required

Directions:

1. After adding the oil to the Instant Pan, ensure that the appliance is established to the Sauté setting.

2. After adding the mushrooms, continue cooking for another five mins.

3. After adding the water and noodles, make sure to mix it thoroughly.

4. Place the cover on the pan, then place it in the oven and cook it on High for five mins.

5. When you are finished, use the rapid release to relieve the pressure.

6. Take off the cover.

7. After stirring in the final components, the dish is ready to be served.

Per servings: Calories: 213kcal; Fat: 17.3g; Carbs: 9.5g; Protein: 7.4g

38. Pecorino Pasta With Sausage and Tomato

Preparation time: twenty mins

Cooking time: 20 mins

Servings: four

Ingredients:

- 1 cup penne pasta
- two teaspoons olive oil
- quarter teaspoon salt
- one cup sliced onion
- one by eighth teaspoon of black pepper
- 8 oz. of Italian sausage
- 1 1/4 lbs. of tomatoes
- 6 tablespoons of aggravated Romano cheese
- quarter cup of torn basil leaves
- 2 teaspoons of garlic

Directions:

1. Pasta should be boiled and then drained.

2. Set aside the cooked pasta.

3. Heat a skillet that should be nonstick over a high flame.

4. Inside a pan, warm the oil and include the sausage & onion—cook for around two mins. Eliminate the pot from the flame, then include the pasta, black pepper powder, salt, and cheese.

5. In a pan, pour the oil and swirl it around to coat it.

6. Offer with the rest of the 1/4 cup of cheese.

Per servings: Calories: 389kcal; Fat: 10g; Carbs: 43g; Protein: 21g

39. Salmon And Couscous

Preparation time: 20 mins

Cooking time: ten mins

Servings: four

Ingredients:

- half cup couscous
- 1 and ½ cups of water
- one tbsp. olive oil
- four salmon fillets, skinless and boneless
- 4 tablespoons tahini paste
- Juice of 1 lemon
- 1 lemon, cut into wedges
- ½ cucumber, chopped
- Seeds from 1 pomegranate
- A small bunch of parsley, chopped

Directions:

1. Place the couscous inside a container, include water, cover and leave away for 8 mins.

2. Heat the oil over medium heat, add salmon, cook for 5 minutes on one side, flip, cook for two more minutes, remove from heat and cast away.

3. Combine tahini with lemon juice and a splash of water in a bowl and whisk well.

4. Drain couscous and the remaining ingredients except for the lemon wedges, and toss and divide between plates.

5. Add the salmon to the couscous and offer using lemon wedges on the end.

Per servings: Calories: 254kcal; Fat: 3g; Carbs: 3g; Protein: 4g

40. Maccheroni With Cherry Tomatoes And Anchovies

Preparation time: 10 minutes

Cooking time: 15 minutes

Servings: 4

Ingredients:

- 6 salted anchovies
- Fresh chili peppers to taste
- 14 oz. of maccheroni pasta
- one clove of garlic
- Salt, as required
- 3 tablespoons of olive oil
- 4 oz. of cherry tomatoes
- 3 basil leaves

Directions:

1. Begin by boiling water inside a saucepan and adding salt after it has reached a boil. Meanwhile, make the sauce by washing the tomatoes and cutting them into four pieces.

2. Now, in a non-stick pan, drizzle a little oil & toss in a garlic clove. Remove it from the pan once it's done cooking. Clean the anchovies and place them in the pan to melt in the oil.

3. When the anchovies are completely dissolved, add the sliced tomato pieces and cook on high flame till they soften.

4. Season with the seeds removed from the chili peppers, sliced into pieces.

5. Transfer the pasta to a pot of boiling water, drain it al dente, and sauté for a few minutes in the saucepan.

6. Serve & enjoy.

Per servings: Calories: 476kcal; Fat: 11g; Carbs: 61g; Protein: 13g

41. Delicious Chicken Pasta

Preparation time: ten mins

Cooking time: 20 mins

Servings: four

Ingredients:

- half cup of sun-dried tomatoes
- three chicken breasts, skinless & boneless, sliced into parts
- Pepper
- 14 ounces can of tomato, diced
- 1 cup of chicken broth
- 9 oz. of whole-grain pasta
- Salt
- 1/2 cup of olives, sliced
- 1 tablespoon of roasted red peppers, chopped
- 2 cups of marinara sauce

Directions:

1. Inside the instant pan, combine the entire components except the whole-grain pasta.

2. Cook for around 12 minutes on high with the lid closed.

3. Allow for natural pressure release after you've finished. Take off the cover.

4. Stir in the spaghetti well. Re-seal the pot and establish the timer for approximately 5 mins on manual.

5. Release the pressure for 5 minutes after finishing, then use the rapid release to release the remaining pressure. Take off the cover. Serve with a good stir.

Per servings: Calories: 615kcal; Fat: 15g; Carbs: 51g; Protein: 48g

42. Pork And Herbed Couscous Mix

Preparation time: 10 minutes

Cooking time: 7 hours

Servings: six

Ingredients:

- two and ½ lbs. pork loin boneless and trimmed
- ¾ cup chicken stock
- two tbsps. olive oil
- half tbsp. sweet paprika
- 2 and ¼ teaspoon sage, dried
- half tbsp. garlic powder
- quarter tsp. rosemary, dried
- quarter tsp. marjoram, dried
- one tsp. basil, dried
- one tsp. oregano, dried
- Salt and black pepper, as required
- 2 cups couscous, cooked

Directions:

1. Mix the pork with oil with stock, paprika, garlic powder, sage, rosemary, thyme, marjoram, oregano, salt, and pepper as required, toss thoroughly and transfer to the slow cooker.

2. Add the rest of the ingredients, stir, cover and cook on Low for 7 hours.

3. Divide between plates and serve with couscous on the side.

Per servings: Calories: 310kcal; Fat: 4g; Carbs: 7g; Protein: 14g

43. Confetti Couscous

Preparation time: 10 minutes

Cooking time: twenty mins

Servings: four to six

Ingredients:

- three tbsp additional-virgin olive oil
- one big onion, sliced
- two carrots, sliced
- one cup fresh peas
- half cup golden raisins
- one tsp salt
- two cups vegetable broth
- two cups couscous

Directions:

1. Sauté the onions, carrots, peas, and raisins for five mins while tossing them all simultaneously in the oil that is in your moderate saucepan and placing it across moderate flame.

2. After adding the salt and the liquid, mix the two ingredients together. Raise to a simmer and continue boiling for another five mins with the components.

3. After adding the couscous, give everything a good toss. Reduce the flame to medium, conceal, and continue cooking for ten mins. To distribute, spread the rice with a spatula.

Per servings: Calories: 511kcal; Fat: 12g; Carbs: 92g; Protein: 14g

44. Sicilian Spaghetti

Preparation time: ten mins

Cooking time: 10 mins

Servings: eight

Ingredients:

- three crushed garlic cloves
- 1 cup parsley

- 4 tablespoons of cheese
- Black pepper to taste
- 1 lb. of whole-wheat spaghetti
- 4 tablespoons of olive oil
- 1 cup of whole-wheat bread crumbs
- 2 oz. of anchovy fillets

Directions:

1. Inside a big deep pot, cook the pasta in boiling water on medium flame for 10 mins.

2. Cook for around three minutes, constantly stirring, in hot olive oil with anchovies and garlic.

3. Inside a mixing bowl, combine the breadcrumbs, pepper, & parsley.

4. Before serving, combine the anchovies with the spaghetti and top using the cheese.

Per servings: Calories: 354kcal; Fat: 10g; Carbs: 43g; Protein: 13g

45. Couscous And Apricots Bowls

Preparation time: 15 mins
Cooking time: 5 mins
Servings: four
Ingredients:

- 3 cups low fat milk
- one cinnamon stick
- ½ cup apricots, dried and chopped
- 1 cup couscous, uncooked
- ¼ cup currants, dried
- A pinch of salt
- 6 teaspoons brown sugar
- 4 teaspoons butter, melted

Directions:

1. Warm a pan with the milk and the cinnamon stick across moderate flame for about 5 mins and take off the heat.

2. Add the couscous and the other ingredients, stir, cover and leave aside for fifteen mins.

3. Discard cinnamon stick, separate into containers and distribute.

Per servings: Calories: 250kcal; Fat: 6.5g; Carbs: 24g; Protein: 10g

46. Broccoli And Tomato Pasta

Preparation time: 15 minutes
Cooking time: 20 minutes
Servings: 4
Ingredients:

- 2 cups of broccoli
- 3 quarts of water
- 2 tablespoons of olive oil
- 1/2 cup of crushed parsley
- two crushed garlic cloves
- 8 oz. spaghetti
- one-eighth tsp. of pepper
- 2 tomatoes chopped
- half cup of olives sliced
- half tsp. red pepper
- quarter cup Romano cheese grated
- 3/4 teaspoon salt

Directions:

1. Inside a pot, raise to a simmer, then include the spaghetti and cook for around five mins. Add broccoli and boil for around three to four mins, or till the pasta & broccoli are both soft.

2. Cook for around 2 minutes inside a nonstick griddle, and fry the tomatoes, garlic, and pepper flakes.

3. Drain the pasta then include it to the griddle. Toss with the rest of the components to cover.

4. Distribute.

Per servings: Calories: 348kcal; Fat: 12g; Carbs: 51g; Protein: 12g

47. Simple Tuna Pasta

Preparation time: 10 mins

Cooking time: ten mins

Servings: two

Ingredients:

- two minced cloves of garlic
- 1 tablespoon of chopped parsley
- 4 oz. of uncooked pasta
- 2 tbsps. olive oil
- 5 oz. tuna
- Black pepper, as required
- 1 teaspoon of lemon juice
- Salt to taste

Directions:

1. Inside a pot of boiling water, cook the pasta for around 7 minutes.

2. Across moderate flame, fry garlic for half a min in heated oil.

3. Combine the tuna, parsley, & lemon juice—cook for an additional min.

4. Include 3 spoonsful of pasta water & combine thoroughly.

5. Toss the drained pasta and mix thoroughly. Serve and have fun!

Per servings: Calories: 400kcal; Fat: 16g; Carbs: 44g; Protein: 21g

48. Cinnamon Couscous And Cauliflower

Preparation time: 10 minutes

Cooking time: 10 minutes

Servings: 4

Ingredients:

- 1 and ½ cups couscous, already cooked
- 3 tablespoons olive oil
- 3 cups cauliflower florets
- one shallot, sliced
- Salt and pepper, as required
- A pinch of cinnamon, ground
- ¼ cup dates, chopped
- A splash of red wine vinegar
- Handful parsley, chopped

Directions:

1. Place cooked couscous in a bowl, add one tablespoon oil, toss to coat and leave aside.

2. Heat a pot using remaining oil across moderate-high flame, include shallot, stir and cook for two mins.

3. Include cauliflower florets, dates, salt, pepper, and cinnamon, mix and cook for 5-6 mins.

4. Add couscous, and the remaining components, whisk, cook for 1 minute, split among plates and distribute.

Per servings: Calories: 345kcal; Fat: 11g; Carbs: 55g; Protein: 9g

49. Turkey And Couscous

Preparation time: 10 minutes

Cooking time: 25 minutes

Servings: 4

Ingredients:

- 1 ½ cups couscous
- ½ cup vegetable oil
- 1 cup breadcrumbs
- 2 cups chicken stock
- 1 tablespoon sesame seeds
- Salt and black pepper, as required
- A tweak of paprika
- A pinch of cayenne pepper
- 2 eggs

- 4 turkey breast cutlets
- ¼ cup parsley, chopped
- 4 ounces feta cheese, crumbled
- ¼ cup red onion, chopped
- ½ cup white flour
- 4 lemon wedges

Directions:

1. Warm up a pot using two tablespoons of oil across moderate-high flame, include couscous, mix, cook for 7 mins, include the stock, raise to a simmer, cook for ten more mins and then cool down for a few minutes.

2. Mix breadcrumbs with sesame seeds, cayenne, paprika, salt, and pepper in a bowl.

3. Whisk eggs well in another bowl and put the flour in a third one.

4. Dredge turkey in flour, eggs, and breadcrumbs.

5. Heat a pan with remaining oil over medium-high heat, add cutlets, cook for 6 minutes, flipping once and transfer them to paper towels to drain excess grease.

6. Mix couscous with parsley and the remaining ingredients except for the lemon, stir, divide between plates, divide the turkey and serve with lemon wedges.

Per servings: Calories: 760kcal; Fat: 20g; Carbs: 34g; Protein: 40g

50. Mediterranean Farfalle

Preparation time: ten mins
Cooking time: 15 mins
Servings: 7
Ingredients:

- quarter cup chopped basil leaves
- one and a quarter cups of farfalle pasta
- ½ cup pine nuts
- 2 chopped garlic cloves
- half cup of olive oil
- ¼ cup of red wine vinegar
- one pound of beaten chorizo sausage
- half cup of tattered parmesan cheese
- 1 cup of diced tomato

Directions:

1. Boil the water with a pinch of salt in a pot.

2. Cook, occasionally stirring, till the pasta is al dente.

3. Cook chorizo inside a pot on moderate flame. Cook for almost five mins after adding the nuts.

4. Remove the pan from the flame after adding the garlic and cooking for a minute.

5. Combine the cooked pasta, vinegar, tomatoes, cheese, cooked chorizo combination, olive oil, and basil inside a large-sized mixing bowl. Serve after thoroughly mixing to coat everything.

Per servings: Calories: 692kcal; Fat: 48g; Carbs: 40g; Protein: 26g

CHAPTER 4: MEAT

51. Grilled Skirt Steak over Hummus	42
52. Seasoned Beef Kebabs	42
53. Rosemary Pork Chops	42
54. Lemon-Simmered Chicken & Artichokes	43
55. Crispy Mediterranean Chicken Thighs	43
56. Greek Lamb Burgers	43
57. Ground Lamb with Lentils and Pomegranate Seeds	44
58. Spanish Pepper Steak	45
59. Braised Veal	45
60. Minty Balsamic Lamb	45
61. Pork Chops and Herbed Tomato Sauce	46
62. Sumac Chicken with Cauliflower and Carrots	46
63. Greek Turkey Burger	47
64. Pork Tenderloin with Dill Sauce	47
65. Walnut Turkey with Peaches	47
66. Orange Duck and Celery	48
67. Roasted Lamb Chops	48
68. Coriander and Coconut Chicken	48
69. Chicken Shawarma	49
70. Beef Cacciatore	49

51. Grilled Skirt Steak over Hummus

Preparation time: ten mins

Cooking time: 13-15 mins

Servings: four

Ingredients:

- one pound skirt steak
- one tsp salt
- ½ tsp freshly ground black pepper
- 2 cups prepared hummus
- 1 tablespoon additional-virgin olive oil
- ½ cup pine nuts

Directions:

1. Preheat a grill over moderate heat.
2. Flavor the steak with salt and pepper on all sides.
3. Cook the steak on each side for 3 to 5 minutes and let it rest for 5 minutes. Slice the meat into thin strips.
4. Spread the hummus on a serving dish and evenly distribute the beef on top of the hummus.
5. Add olive oil and pine nuts to your small pot across low flame. Toast them for three mins, stirring them with a spoon, so they don't burn.
6. Spoon the pine nuts over the beef and serve.

Per servings: Calories: 602kcal; Fat: 41g; Carbs: 20g; Protein: 42g

52. Seasoned Beef Kebabs

Preparation time: fifteen mins

Cooking time: 10 mins

Servings: six

Ingredients:

- 2 lbs. beef fillet
- one and a half tsps. salt
- one teaspoon freshly ground black pepper
- half teaspoon ground allspice
- ½ teaspoon ground nutmeg
- 1/3 cup extra-virgin olive oil
- 1 large onion, cut into 8 quarters
- 1 large red bell pepper, sliced into 1-inch cubes

Directions:

1. Preheat a grill, grill pan, or lightly oiled skillet to high heat.
2. Cut the beef into 1-inch cubes and put them in a large bowl.
3. Inside a small container, combine the salt, black pepper, allspice, and nutmeg.
4. Pour the olive oil over the beef and toss to coat the beef. Evenly sprinkle the seasoning over the beef and toss to coat all pieces.
5. Skewer the beef, alternating every 1 or 2 pieces with a piece of onion or bell pepper.
6. To cook, place the skewers on the grill or skillet and turn every 2 to 3 minutes until all sides have cooked to desired doneness, 6 minutes for medium-rare, 8 minutes for well done. Serve warm.

Per servings: Calories: 485kcal; Fat: 36g; Carbs: 4g; Protein: 35g

53. Rosemary Pork Chops

Preparation time: 10 minutes

Cooking time: 35 minutes

Servings: 4

Ingredients:

- 4 pork loin chops, boneless
- 4 garlic cloves, crushed
- one tablespoon rosemary, sliced
- one tablespoon olive oil
- Salt & black pepper, as required

Directions:

1. Mix the pork chops and remaining ingredients in a roasting pan. Bake in the microwave around 425 deg. F for ten mins.

2. Adjust the flame to 350 deg. F and cook the chops for 25 minutes more. Serve.

Per servings: Calories: 161kcal; Fat: 5g; Carbs: 1g; Protein: 25g

54. Lemon-Simmered Chicken & Artichokes

Preparation time: 10 minutes

Cooking time: 10-15 minutes

Servings: 4

Ingredients:

- 4 boneless chicken breast halves, skins removed
- 1/4 tsp Himalayan salt
- 1/4 tsp freshly ground black pepper
- 2 tsp avocado oil
- 1 tablespoon lemon juice
- two tsps. dried crushed oregano
- quarter cup olives, pitted and halved
- 2/3 cup reduced-sodium chicken stock
- 14 oz canned, water-packed, quartered artichoke hearts

Directions:

1. Sprinkle the chicken with salt and pepper. Brown the chicken in a pan for 2 to 4 minutes.

2. Add the chicken stock, oregano, olives, lemon juice, and artichoke hearts. Stir well and let it boil. Cover, adjust to a simmer for 4-5 minutes, and serve hot.

Per servings: Calories: 225kcal; Fat: 9g; Carbs: 9g; Protein: 2g

55. Crispy Mediterranean Chicken Thighs

Preparation time: 10 mins

Cooking time: 30-35 mins

Servings: six

Ingredients:

- two tbsp additional-virgin olive oil
- two tsp dried rosemary
- one and a half tsp ground cumin
- one and a half tsp ground coriander
- ¾ tsp dried oregano
- one by eighth tsp salt
- six chicken thighs, bone-in, & skin-on

Directions:

1. Turn the microwave temperature up to 450 degrees Fahrenheit. A baking sheet with parchment paper should be prepared.

2. To make a paste, combine the seasonings with the olive oil inside a big container and stir until combined. After adding the poultry, continue to combine till it is completely covered. Place on the previously prepared baking sheet.

3. Bake 30 to 35 mins until golden brown.

Per servings: Calories: 440kcal; Fat: 34g; Carbs: 1g; Protein: 30g

56. Greek Lamb Burgers

Preparation time: 10 minutes

Cooking time: 6-10 minutes

Servings: 4

Ingredients:

- 1-pound ground lamb
- ½ tsp salt
- ½ tsp freshly ground black pepper
- 4 tbsp feta cheese, crumbled
- Buns for serving (optional)

Directions:

1. Preheat a grill, grill pan, or lightly oiled skillet to high heat.

2. Using your hands, combine the lamb with the salt and pepper in a large bowl.

3. Divide the meat into 4 portions. Divide each portion in half and flatten every half into a 3-inch circle.

4. Make a dent in the center of one of the halves and place 1 tbsp feta cheese in the center.

5. Place the second half of the patty on top of the feta cheese and press down to close the 2 halves together, making it resemble a round burger.

6. Cook the stuffed patty for 3 mins on every end for moderate-well. Serve on a bun, if desired.

Per servings: Calories: 345kcal; Fat: 29g; Carbs: 1g; Protein: 20g

57. Ground Lamb with Lentils and Pomegranate Seeds

Preparation time: fifteen mins
Cooking time: fifteen to eighteen mins
Servings: four
Ingredients:

- one tbsp additional-virgin olive oil
- half lb. ground lamb
- one tsp red pepper flakes
- ½ tsp ground cumin
- ½ tsp kosher salt
- ¼ tsp freshly ground black pepper
- two garlic cloves, crushed
- two cups cooked, wearied lentils
- one hothouse or English cucumber, chopped
- one-third cup fresh mint, sliced
- one-third cup fresh parsley, sliced
- Zest of one lemon
- one cup plain Greek yogurt
- half cup pomegranate seeds

Directions:

1. The oil should be heated in a sauté skillet that is set across moderate-high flame. After adding the lamb, top it via cumin, crushed red pepper flakes, salt, and ground black pepper.

2. After five mins of cooking despite being stirred, the underside of the lamb should be browned and crispy. Continue stirring, and continue cooking for an additional five mins.

3. Make the lamb into smaller chunks by tearing it apart with a spatula. After adding the garlic, continue cooking for another min while turning it periodically. Place the lamb mixture in a dish that is about moderate in size.

4. After adding the lentils to the pan, cook them for five mins, tossing them periodically, till they are browned and crisp.

5. Place the lamb back into the saucepan, give everything a good stir, and allow it to reheat for three mins. Move the mixture into the big basin.

6. Combine by combining the cucumber, mint, parsley, and lemon juice in a gentle manner.

7. Place a few yoghurt in every one of the containers, then cover them all with a portion of the lamb mixture. Pomegranate seeds should be sprinkled on top as a garnish.

Per servings: Calories: 370kcal; Fat: 18g; Carbs: 30g; Protein: 24g

58. Spanish Pepper Steak

Preparation time: 10 minutes

Cooking time: 20 minutes

Servings: 4

Ingredients:

- 1-pound beef fillet
- 1 tbsp smoked paprika
- ¼ cup extra-virgin olive oil
- 3 tbsp garlic, minced
- 1½ tsp salt
- 1 large onion, sliced
- 2 large bell peppers, any color, sliced

Directions:

8. Season the meat with paprika and cut it into thin slices.

9. Inside a big griddle, cook the olive oil, garlic, beef, and salt for 7 mins over medium heat.

10. Adjust to low heat and include the onion afterwards cook for 7 mins. Include the bell peppers and cook for 6 minutes. Serve.

Per servings: Calories: 441kcal; Fat: 32g; Carbs: 12g; Protein: 28g

59. Braised Veal

Preparation time: ten mins

Cooking time: 2 hours

Servings: four

Ingredients:

- four veal shanks, bone-in
- ½ cup flour
- 4 tbsps. additional-virgin olive oil
- one big onion, sliced
- 5 cloves garlic, sliced
- two tsp salt
- 1 tbsp fresh thyme
- 3 tbsp tomato paste
- 6 cups water
- Cooked noodles for serving (optional)

Directions:

1. Preheat the oven to 350 deg. F.

2. Dredge the veal shanks in the flour.

3. Heat a large oven-safe pan with olive oil over medium heat. Cook the veal shanks on both sides for 8 minutes. Remove the veal and cast it away.

4. Include the onion, garlic, salt, thyme, and tomato paste to the pan and cook for 3 to 4 minutes. Add the water and stir to combine.

5. Add the veal back to your pan and let it simmer. Conceal and bake for one hr and 50 mins.

6. Eliminate from the microwave and distribute with cooked noodles, if desired.

Per servings: Calories: 400kcal; Fat: 19g; Carbs: 18g; Protein: 39g

60. Minty Balsamic Lamb

Preparation time: 10 minutes

Cooking time: 11 minutes

Servings: 4

Ingredients:

- 2 red chilies, chopped
- 2 tbsp balsamic vinegar
- 1 cup mint leaves, chopped
- 2 tbsp olive oil
- 4 lamb fillets
- 1 tbsp sweet paprika
- Salt & black pepper, as required

Directions:

1. Warm up a pot with half the oil across moderate-high flame and include all the ingredients, except the lamb. Whisk it well and cook across moderate flame for five mins.

2. After giving the lamb a light coating of the remainder of the oil and seasoning using salt and black pepper, position it on the grill after it has been warmed up and cook it for three mins on every end across moderate flame.

3. Split the lamb among plates, drizzle the minty vinaigrette, and serve.

Per servings: Calories: 312kcal; Fat: 12g; Carbs: 17g; Protein: 17g

61. Pork Chops and Herbed Tomato Sauce

Preparation time: 10 minutes
Cooking time: 12 minutes
Servings: 4
Ingredients:
- 4 pork loin chops, boneless
- 6 tomatoes, peeled & crushed
- 3 tbsp parsley, chopped
- 2 tbsp olive oil
- ¼ cup kalamata olives pitted & halved
- 1 yellow onion, chopped
- 1 garlic clove, minced

Directions:

1. Heat a pot using the oil. Include the pork chops, cook 3 mins on every end, and split them among plates.

2. Warm the same pot over moderate flame and include the tomatoes, parsley, and remaining ingredients. Whisk well, simmer for 4 minutes, drizzle over the chops, and serve.

Per servings: Calories: 334kcal; Fat: 17g; Carbs: 12g; Protein: 34g

62. Sumac Chicken with Cauliflower and Carrots

Preparation time: fifteen mins
Cooking time: forty mins
Servings: four
Ingredients:
- 3 tbsp additional-virgin olive oil
- 1 tbsp ground sumac
- 1 tsp kosher salt
- ½ tsp ground cumin
- ¼ tsp freshly ground black pepper
- one and a half lbs. bone-in chicken thighs & drumsticks
- 1 average cauliflower, sliced into one inch florets
- 2 carrots, skinned & sliced into one inch rounds
- 1 lemon, sliced into quarter inch-dense pieces
- 1 tbsp lemon juice
- quarter cup fresh parsley, sliced
- quarter cup fresh mint, sliced

Directions:

1. Warm the microwave to 425 deg. F. Line your baking sheet using parchment paper.

2. Whisk the olive oil, sumac, salt, cumin, and black pepper in a big container.

3. Swirl the chicken, cauliflower, and carrots in the oil and spice combination till the poultry, cauliflower, and carrots are completely covered.

4. Place a single layer of the poultry, cauliflower, and carrots on the baking sheet. Lemon segments should be placed on the surface.

5. Roast the vegetables for forty mins, turning them over briefly midway by means of the cooking time. The poultry and vegetables should be seasoned with the lemon juice, and the dish should be garnished with fresh parsley and mint.

Per servings: Calories: 510kcal; Fat: 38g; Carbs: 13g; Protein: 31g

63. Greek Turkey Burger

Preparation time: 15 mins

Cooking time: ten mins

Servings: four

Ingredients:

- one lb. ground turkey
- one average zucchini, aggravated
- quarter cup whole-wheat bread crumbs
- quarter cup red onion, crushed
- quarter cup smashed feta cheese
- one big egg, whisked
- one garlic clove, crushed
- one tbsp fresh oregano, sliced
- one tsp kosher salt
- ¼ tsp freshly ground black pepper
- one tbsp additional-virgin olive oil

Directions:

1. Mix the ground turkey, zucchini, bread crumbs, onion, feta cheese, egg, garlic, oregano, and salt and pepper to taste in a big dish until everything is evenly distributed. Form into four similar burgers.

2. Olive oil should be heated across moderate-high flame inside a big nonstick griddle pot or griddle. Put the burgers in the pot, and regulate the flame so that it is moderate.

3. Cook for five mins on one end, afterwards turn and continue cooking for an additional five mins on the other end.

Per servings: Calories: 285kcal; Fat: 16g; Carbs: 9g; Protein: 26g

64. Pork Tenderloin with Dill Sauce

Preparation time: ten mins

Cooking time: twenty mins

Servings: four

Ingredients:

- one lb. pork tenderloin, sliced
- 3 tbsp coriander seeds, ground
- 2 tbsp olive oil
- 1/3 cup heavy cream
- ½ cup dill, chopped
- Salt & black pepper to taste

Directions:

1. Warm a pot with the oil across moderate-high flame. Cook the pork four mins on every end.

2. Include the remaining ingredients, let it simmer, and cook over medium heat for 12 minutes more. Divide it between plates and serve.

Per servings: Calories: 320kcal; Fat: 14g; Carbs: 13g; Protein: 17g

65. Walnut Turkey with Peaches

Preparation time: 10 minutes

Cooking time: 60 minutes

Servings: 4

Ingredients:

- 2 turkey breasts, skinless, boneless & sliced
- ¼ cup chicken stock
- 1 tbsp walnuts, chopped
- 1 red onion, chopped
- 2 tbsp olive oil
- 4 peaches, pitted and cut into quarters
- 1 tbsp cilantro, chopped
- Salt & black pepper to taste

Directions:

1. In a roasting pan greased with the oil, combine the turkey and the remaining ingredients, except for the cilantro.

2. Bake in the microwave at 390 deg. F for one hr; divide the mix between plates, sprinkle the cilantro on top, and serve.

Per servings: Calories: 500kcal; Fat: 14g; Carbs: 15g; Protein: 10g

66. Orange Duck and Celery

Preparation time: ten mins

Cooking time: 40 mins

Servings: 4

Ingredients:

- two duck legs, boneless, & skinless
- 1 tbsp avocado oil
- one cup chicken stock
- Salt & black pepper, as required
- 4 celery ribs, roughly chopped
- two garlic cloves, crushed
- one red onion, sliced
- two teaspoon thyme, dried
- 2 tbsp tomato paste
- Zest of one orange, aggravated
- Juice of 2 oranges
- 3 oranges, peeled & cut into segments

Directions:

1. Oil a roasting pot using the oil and add the duck legs and remaining components.

2. Toss it well and bake in the microwave at 450 deg. F for forty mins. Split everything among plates and offer warm.

Per servings: Calories: 294kcal; Fat: 12g; Carbs: 25g; Protein: 16g

67. Roasted Lamb Chops

Preparation time: ten mins

Cooking time: 27 mins

Servings: four

Ingredients:

- 4 lamb chops
- ½ cup basil leaves, sliced
- half cup mint leaves, sliced
- one tbsp rosemary, sliced
- two garlic cloves, crushed
- two tbsps. olive oil
- one eggplant, cubed
- two zucchinis, cubed
- 1 yellow bell pepper, roughly chopped
- 2 oz feta cheese, crumbled
- 8 oz cherry tomatoes, halved

Directions:

1. Combine the pork chops with the rest of the components in a roasting pan and conceal with tin foil.

2. Bake in the microwave and bake at 400 deg. F for 27 mins. Split it among plates and distribute.

Per servings: Calories: 334kcal; Fat: 17g; Carbs: 18g; Protein: 24g

68. Coriander and Coconut Chicken

Preparation time: 10 minutes

Cooking time: 28-30 minutes

Servings: 4

Ingredients:

- 2 pounds chicken thighs, skinless, boneless & cubed
- two tbsps. olive oil
- 3 tbsps. coconut flesh, shredded
- one and a half tsp orange extract

- 1 tbsp ginger, grated
- ¼ cup orange juice
- two tbsps. coriander, sliced
- one cup chicken stock
- quarter teaspoon red pepper flakes
- Salt & black pepper, as required

Directions:

1. Place the oil in a skillet and bring it up to a moderate-high flame. Cook the chicken for four mins per end in the pot.

2. Sprinkle in the salt, pepper, and the remaining components, then raise to a boil before reducing the heat to moderate and cooking for another twenty mins. The mixture should be served warm and should be divided among several dishes.

Per servings: Calories: 297kcal; Fat: 14g; Carbs: 22g; Protein: 25g

69. Chicken Shawarma

Preparation time: 20 minutes
Cooking time: twelve mins
Servings: 2-4
Ingredients:

- one lb. chicken, boneless & skinless, sliced into ¼-inch pieces
- quarter cup extra-virgin olive oil
- 1/4 cup lemon juice
- 1 1/2 tbsp minced garlic
- 3/4 tsp salt
- 1/8 tsp each of freshly ground black pepper, ground cardamom & cinnamon

For serving:

- Hummus & pita bread, if desired

Directions:

1. Put the chicken strips into a large container.

2. Whisk the lemon juice, oil, garlic, salt, pepper, cardamom, and cinnamon in a separate bowl.

3. Place the dressing across the chicken and stir to cover all the chicken. Let it sit for about 10 minutes.

4. Place your large pot across moderate-high flame and brown the chicken strips for 12 mins.

5. Serve with hummus and pita bread, if desired.

Per servings: Calories: 477kcal; Fat: 32g; Carbs: 5g; Protein: 47g

70. Beef Cacciatore

Preparation time: 10 minutes
Cooking time: 50 minutes
Servings: 5
Ingredients:

- 1 pound beef, cut into thin slices
- ¼ cup extra-virgin olive oil
- one onion, sliced
- 2 red bell peppers, chopped
- 1 orange bell pepper, chopped
- Salt & pepper, to taste
- 1 cup tomato sauce

Directions:

1. Heat your skillet with oil over medium heat and cook the beef until browned.

2. Cook the onions and peppers for three-five mins. Include the tomato sauce, salt, and pepper then mix thoroughly. Let it simmer.

3. Cover and cook for 40 mins till the meat is softer. Pour as much sauce as possible then whizz in a blender.

4. Put it back into the pot and heat again for 5 mins. Offer with pasta or rice and enjoy.

Per servings: Calories: 428kcal; Fat: 35g; Carbs: 16g; Protein: 12g

Chapter 5
Fish & Seafood

71. Sesame Shrimp Mix	51
72. Baked Salmon with Garlic Cilantro Sauce	51
73. Salmon and Corn Salad	51
74. Cod and Mushrooms Mix	52
75. Shrimp with White Beans and Feta	52
76. Marinated Tuna Steak	53
77. Garlic and Shrimp Pasta	53
78. Cod and Cauliflower Chowder	54
79. Calamari and Dill Sauce	54
80. White Wine–Sautéed Mussels	54
81. Chopped Tuna Salad	55
82. Tuna & Bean Wraps	55
83. Flounder with Tomatoes and Basil	55
84. Salmon and Peach Pan	56
85. Smoked Salmon and Watercress Salad	56
86. Salmon and Broccoli	56
87. Tarragon Cod Fillets	57
88. Cinnamon-Glazed Halibut Fillets	57
89. Seared Scallops with Blood Orange Glaze	57
90. Salmon and Radish Mix	58

71. Sesame Shrimp Mix

Preparation time: ten mins

Cooking time: zero mins

Servings: four

Ingredients:

- two tablespoon lime juice
- 3 tablespoons teriyaki sauce
- 2 tablespoons olive oil
- 8 cups baby spinach
- 14 ounces shrimp, cooked, peeled, and deveined
- 1 cup cucumber, sliced
- 1 cup radish, sliced
- ¼ cup cilantro, chopped
- 2 teaspoons sesame seeds, toasted

Directions:

1. Inside a container, combine the shrimp alongside the lime juice, spinach, and the remaining components, whisk and offer cold.

Per servings: Calories: 173kcal; Fat: 9g; Carbs: 7.58g; Protein: 17g

72. Baked Salmon with Garlic Cilantro Sauce

Preparation time: 10 minutes

Cooking time: 15 minutes

Serving: 6

Ingredients:

- 2 pounds salmon fillet, skinless, frozen, thawed
- 1 large tomato, sliced into rounds
- 5 teaspoons chopped garlic
- 1 cup stems trimmed cilantro, fresh
- ½ large lime, sliced into rounds
- ¼ tsp. ground black pepper
- quarter tsp. salt, divided
- ½ cup olive oil
- 3 tablespoons lime juice

Directions:

1. Switch on the oven, set the temperature to 425 degrees F, or 218 degrees C, and let it preheat.

2. Meanwhile, take a large baking pan, spray it with cooking spray to grease it, and then set it aside until required.

3. Plugin a food processor, add garlic, cilantro, salt, oil, lime juice, and pulse until well mixed.

4. Then transfer the prepared cilantro and garlic sauce into a small bowl, and set it aside until required.

5. Place the salmon fillet onto the prepared baking pan, and sprinkle salt and black pepper all around to season it.

6. Then spoon the prepared sauce on top of the salmon, spread it evenly until coated, and place the tomato slices, and lime slices on top.

7. Place the baking pan on the second shelf of the microwave, and bake for 5 mins, or till almost done.

8. Then, conceal the baking pot with aluminum foil, and bake for another 7 mins, or 'til cooked.

9. When done, place the prepared salmon on a serving plate, and serve immediately.

Per servings: Calories: 302kcal; Fat: 16.7g; Carbs: 5.4g; Protein: 34.4g

73. Salmon and Corn Salad

Preparation time: five mins

Cooking time: zero mins

Servings: four

Ingredients:

- half cup pecans, chopped
- 2 cups baby arugula
- 1 cup corn
- ¼ pound smoked salmon, skinless, boneless, and cut into small chunks

- 2 tablespoons olive oil
- 2 tablespoon lemon juice
- Sea salt and black pepper to the taste

Directions:

1. Within a salad container, combine the salmon with the corn and the remaining components, whisk, and offer right away.

Per servings: Calories: 228kcal; Fat: 18.7g; Carbs: 10g; Protein: 8.1g

74. Cod and Mushrooms Mix

Preparation time: ten mins
Cooking time: 25 mins
Servings: 4
Ingredients:

- two cod fillets, boneless
- 4 tablespoons olive oil
- 4 ounces mushrooms, sliced
- Sea salt and black pepper to the taste
- 12 cherry tomatoes, halved
- 8 ounces lettuce leaves, torn
- 1 avocado, pitted, skinned, and chopped
- one red chili pepper, sliced
- one tbsp. cilantro, sliced
- 2 tablespoons balsamic vinegar
- one oz. feta cheese, beaten

Directions:

1. Placing the fish in a roasting pot, brushing it with two tbsps. of oil, sprinkling it via salt and pepper completely, and then broiling it for fifteen mins in moderate-high flame are all good ways to cook fish. In the meantime, warm the remaining oil in a skillet across moderate flame, include the mushrooms, and fry them for five mins whilst stirring occasionally.

2. Whisk in the remaining components, cook for an additional five mins, and then distribute the dish among the plates.

3. Top with the fish and serve right away.

Per servings: Calories: 283kcal; Fat: 20.7g; Carbs: 9.4g; Protein: 17g

75. Shrimp with White Beans and Feta

Preparation time: fifteen mins
Cooking time: 7-15 mins
Servings: four
Ingredients:

- three tbsp lemon juice, separated
- two tbsp additional-virgin olive oil, separated
- ½ tsp kosher salt, separated
- one lb. shrimp, skinned and deveined
- one big shallot, cubed
- ¼ cup no-salt-included vegetable stock
- one (fifteen oz) can of no-salt-included or low-sodium cannellini beans, washed and wearied
- quarter cup fresh mint, sliced
- one tsp lemon zest
- one tbsp white wine vinegar
- ¼ tsp freshly ground black pepper
- quarter cup beaten feta cheese for garnish

Directions:

1. Whisk one tbsp lemon juice, one tbsp olive oil, and ¼ tsp salt inside a small container. Include the shrimp and set aside.

2. Heat the skillet over medium heat with the remaining oil. Sauté the shallot for 2 to 3 minutes until translucent.

3. Add the vegetable stock, deglaze the pan, and let it boil. Add the beans and shrimp.

4. Adjust to low heat, cover, and simmer for three-four mins till the shrimp are cooked completely.

5. After the flame has been turned off, stir in the mint, the lemon juice, the vinegar, and the black pepper. To incorporate, give it a light toss. Serve with feta crumbles sprinkled on top.

Per servings: Calories: 340kcal; Fat: 11g; Carbs: 28g; Protein: 32g

76. Marinated Tuna Steak

Preparation time: 6 mins

Cooking time: 18 mins

Servings: four

Ingredients:

- Olive oil (two tbsps.)
- Orange juice (quarter cup)
- Soy sauce (quarter cup)
- Lemon juice (one tablespoon)
- Fresh parsley (two tbsps.)
- Garlic clove (one)
- Ground black pepper (half teaspoon)
- Fresh oregano (half teaspoon)
- Tuna steaks (four - four ounces Steaks)

Directions:

1. Garlic should be minced, and oregano and parsley should be chopped.

2. Combine the pepper, oregano, garlic, parsley, lemon juice, soy sauce, olive oil, and citrus juice inside a bowl made of glass.

3. Prepare the griddle for use by turning the warm it up to high. Apply oil to the grate to make it slippery.

4. Cook for an additional 5 to 6 mins after adding to the tuna fillets. After turning the meat, slather it with the marinade.

5. Continue cooking for a further 5 mins, or till the dish reaches the desired consistency. Throw away the marinate that is left over.

Per servings: Calories: 122kcal; Fat: 8.5g; Carbs: 3.69g; Protein: 8g

77. Garlic and Shrimp Pasta

Preparation time: 4 minutes

Cooking time: 16 minutes

Servings: 4

Ingredients:

- 6 ounces whole-wheat spaghetti
- 12 ounces raw shrimp, skinned and deveined, sliced into one inch pieces
- one bunch asparagus, trimmed
- 1 large bell pepper, thinly sliced
- 1 cup fresh peas
- 3 garlic cloves, chopped
- 1 and ¼ teaspoons kosher salt
- ½ and ½ cups non-fat plain yogurt
- 3 tbsp. lemon juice
- one tablespoon additional-virgin olive oil
- half tsp. fresh ground black pepper
- ¼ cup pine nuts, toasted

Directions:

1. Use a big-sized pan and bring water to a boil.

2. Include your spaghetti and cook them for about minutes less than the directed package instruction.

3. Add shrimp, bell pepper, asparagus and cook for almost 2- 4 mins till the shrimp are softer.

4. Drain the pasta and the contents well.

5. Take a large bowl and mash garlic until a paste form.

6. Whisk in yogurt, parsley, oil, pepper, and lemon juice into the garlic paste.

7. Add pasta mixture and toss well.

8. Serve by sprinkling some pine nuts!

Per servings: Calories: 368.2kcal; Fat: 11.7g; Carbs: 45.9g; Protein: 24.5g

78. Cod and Cauliflower Chowder

Preparation time: fifteen mins

Cooking time: 37-40 mins

Servings: four

Ingredients:

- two tbsp additional-virgin olive oil
- 1 leek, white & light green parts only, cut in half lengthwise and sliced thinly
- 4 garlic cloves, sliced
- 1 medium head cauliflower, coarsely chopped
- 1 tsp kosher salt
- ¼ tsp freshly ground black pepper
- two pints cherry tomatoes
- two cups of no-salt-included vegetable stock
- quarter cup green olives, pitted and sliced
- 1 to 1½ pounds of cod
- ¼ cup fresh parsley, minced

Directions:

1. Warm the oil in your large pot across moderate flame. Include the leek and fry for five mins till lightly golden brown.

2. Include the garlic and sauté 30 seconds. Add the cauliflower, salt, and black pepper and sauté for two-three mins.

3. Include the tomatoes and vegetable stock, adjust to high flame, and let it boil. Adjust to low heat and boil for ten mins.

4. Include the olives and combine them. Include the fish, cover, and simmer for 20 minutes until the fish flakes easily. Gently mix in the parsley.

Per servings: Calories: 270kcal; Fat: 9g; Carbs: 19g; Protein: 30g

79. Calamari and Dill Sauce

Preparation time: 10 mins

Cooking time: fifteen mins

Servings: 4

Ingredients:

- one and a half pound calamari, sliced into rings
- 10 garlic cloves, crushed
- two tbsps. olive oil
- Juice of one & ½ lime
- 2 tbsp balsamic vinegar
- 3 tbsp dill, sliced
- A tweak of salt & black pepper

Directions:

1. Heat a pot with the oil over moderate-high flame, include the garlic, lime juice, and remaining components, except for the calamari, and cook for five mins.

2. Include the calamari rings, cook everything for 10 minutes more, divide between plates, and serve.

Per servings: Calories: 282kcal; Fat: 18g; Carbs: 9g; Protein: 18g

80. White Wine–Sautéed Mussels

Preparation time: 15 mins

Cooking time: ten mins

Servings: two

Ingredients:

- one and a half pounds live mussels
- 1 finely chopped shallot
- one cup dry white wine
- one tbsp minced garlic
- 2 tbsp salted butter

Directions:

1. Scrub the mussel shells to ensure they are clean; trim off any with a beard (hanging string). Put the

mussels inside a big container of water, discarding any that are not tightly closed.

2. Cook the butter, shallots, and garlic for 2 minutes in your large pot across moderate flame. Include the wine and cook for a min.

3. Add the mussels to the pot, toss with the sauce, and cover with a lid. Let it cook for 7 minutes. Discard any mussels that have not opened. Serve in bowls with the wine broth.

Per servings: Calories: 777kcal; Fat: 27g; Carbs: 29g; Protein: 82g

81. Chopped Tuna Salad

Preparation time: 15 mins

Cooking time: zero mins

Servings: four

Ingredients:

- two tbsp extra-virgin olive oil
- two tbsp lemon juice
- 2 tsp Dijon mustard
- ½ teaspoon kosher salt
- quarter teaspoon freshly ground black pepper
- 12 olives, pitted and chopped
- ½ cup celery, diced
- ½ cup red onion, diced
- ½ cup red bell pepper, diced
- ½ cup fresh parsley, sliced
- 2 (6-oz) cans of no-salt-added tuna packed in water, drained
- 6 cups baby spinach

Directions:

1. Mix all the fixings, except for the spinach, in a huge salad bowl until well combined.

2. Divide the spinach evenly among 4 plates or bowls. Spoon the tuna salad evenly on top of the spinach.

Per servings: Calories: 220kcal; Fat: 11g; Carbs: 7g; Protein: 25g

82. Tuna & Bean Wraps

Preparation time: ten mins

Cooking time: 0 mins

Servings: four

Ingredients:

- 1 (15 ounces) canned cannellini beans drained and rinsed
- 1 (12 oz) canned (drained and flaked) light tuna in water
- 1/8 tsp white pepper
- 1/8 tsp kosher salt
- 1 tbsp fresh parsley, chopped
- 2 tbsp extra-virgin avocado oil
- ¼ cup red onion, chopped
- 12 romaine lettuce leaves
- 1 medium-sized ripe Hass avocado, sliced

Directions:

1. Mix the beans, tuna, pepper, salt, parsley, avocado oil, and red onions in a bowl.

2. Spoon some of the mixtures onto each lettuce leaf and top with the sliced avocado before folding. Serve!

Per servings: Calories: 279kcal; Fat: 13g; Carbs: 19g; Protein: 22g

83. Flounder with Tomatoes and Basil

Preparation time: ten mins

Cooking time: 15-20 mins

Servings: four

Ingredients:

- four (5- to 6-oz) flounder fillets
- 1-pound cherry tomatoes
- 4 garlic cloves, sliced

- 2 tbsps. additional-virgin olive oil
- 2 tbsps. lemon juice
- 2 tbsps. basil, cut into ribbons
- ½ teaspoon kosher salt
- quarter teaspoon freshly ground black pepper

Directions:

1. Warm up the microwave to 425 deg. F.

2. Inside a baking dish, combine the tomatoes, garlic, olive oil, lemon juice, basil, salt, and black pepper.

3. Bake for 5 minutes; remove the baking dish and arrange the flounder on top.

4. Bake 10 to 15 minutes until the fish is opaque and begins to flake, depending on its thickness. Serve.

Per servings: Calories: 215kcal; Fat: 9g; Carbs: 6g; Protein: 28g

84. Salmon and Peach Pan

Preparation time: ten mins
Cooking time: 11 mins
Servings: four
Ingredients:

- one tablespoon balsamic vinegar
- one teaspoon thyme, chopped
- one tbsp. ginger, grated
- 2 tbsps. olive oil
- Sea salt and black pepper to the taste
- 3 peaches, cut into medium wedges
- 4 salmon fillets, boneless

Directions:

1. The oil should be heated in a skillet across moderate-high flame before being added to the salmon, which should then be cooked for three mins on every end.

2. Cook for an additional five mins after adding the vinegar, the peaches, and the remaining components, and then distribute the mixture evenly among plates to offer.

Per servings: Calories: 325.8kcal; Fat: 21.4g; Carbs: 9.3g; Protein: 25g

85. Smoked Salmon and Watercress Salad

Preparation time: five mins
Cooking time: zero mins
Servings: four
Ingredients:

- two bunches watercress
- one lb. smoked salmon, skinless, boneless, and flaked
- 2 teaspoons mustard
- ¼ cup lemon juice
- ½ cup Greek yogurt
- Salt and black pepper, as required
- one big cucumber, sliced
- two tbsps. chives, sliced

Directions:

1. Salmon, watercress, and the remaining components should be tossed together in a salad dish, and then the salad should be served as soon as possible.

Per servings: Calories: 181.7kcal; Fat: 6.4g; Carbs: 5.56g; Protein: 25.8g

86. Salmon and Broccoli

Preparation time: ten mins
Cooking time: 20 mins
Servings: four
Ingredients:

- two tbsps. balsamic vinegar
- one broccoli head, florets divided
- four parts of salmon fillets, skinless
- one large red onion, roughly chopped

- one tbsp. olive oil
- Sea salt and black pepper, as required

Directions:

1. Place the salmon, broccoli, as well as the remaining components within a baking dish. Place the dish in the microwave and roast at 390 degrees Fahrenheit for twenty mins.

2. After dividing the mixture among the dishes, offer the dish.

Per servings: Calories: 278kcal; Fat: 17.7g; Carbs: 4.1g; Protein: 25.3g

87. Tarragon Cod Fillets

Preparation time: ten mins
Cooking time: 13 mins
Servings: four
Ingredients:

- four cod fillets, boneless
- ¼ cup capers, drained
- 1 tbsp tarragon, chopped
- 2 tbsp olive oil
- 2 tbsp parsley, chopped
- 1 tbsp olive oil
- 1 tbsp lemon juice
- Sea salt & black pepper, as required

Directions:

1. The oil should be heated in a skillet across moderate-high flame before being added to the fish, which should then be cooked for three mins on every end.

2. Cook for an additional seven mins after adding the remaining ingredients. Split among dishes and distribute.

Per servings: Calories: 162kcal; Fat: 9g; Carbs: 12g; Protein: 16g

88. Cinnamon-Glazed Halibut Fillets

Preparation time: 10 minutes
Cooking time: 20-21 minutes
Servings: 4
Ingredients:

- 1/4 cup extra-virgin avocado oil
- three-quarter teaspoon ground cumin
- half teaspoon white pepper, divided
- half teaspoon kosher salt, divided
- half teaspoon ground cinnamon
- one and a half tbsp capers, drained
- 15 oz canned diced tomatoes, drained
- 4 halibut fillets

Directions:

1. Place the oil in a pan. Add the cumin and fry for about 1 minute or until fragrant.

2. Stir in quarter teaspoon pepper, quarter teaspoon salt, cinnamon, capers, and canned tomatoes. Stir the sauce for about 10 minutes or until it thickens.

3. Pat the fish dry and top it using the remaining salt and pepper. Cover the pan and nestle the seasoned fillets in the simmering sauce.

4. Allow the fish to simmer for 8–10 minutes until it flakes easily. Plate the fish and serve immediately, with the sauce ladled over the cooked fish.

Per servings: Calories: 309kcal; Fat: 14g; Carbs: 5g; Protein: 40g

89. Seared Scallops with Blood Orange Glaze

Preparation time: ten mins
Cooking time: 22-23 mins
Servings: four
Ingredients:

- three tbsp additional-virgin olive oil, split
- three garlic cloves, crushed

- ½ tsp kosher salt, shared
- four blood oranges, juiced
- one tsp blood orange zest
- ½ tsp red pepper flakes
- one lb. scallops, small side muscle eliminated
- ¼ tsp freshly ground black pepper
- quarter cup fresh chives, sliced

Directions:

1. Within a small pot, bring one tablespoon of oil up to temperature across moderate-high flame. Fry the garlic for thirty secs after adding a quarter of a teaspoon of salt to the pan.

2. After adding the orange juice and zest, bring the mixture to a simmer, then decrease the flame to moderate-low and continue to cook for approximately twenty mins, or till the liquid is reduced by approximately halfway.

3. Remove the pan from the flame and stir in the crushed red pepper.

4. After utilizing your paper towel to pat the scallops dry, top them with the rest of the quarter teaspoon of salt and the ground black pepper.

5. Within your big saucepan, bring the oil you have left over to a moderate-high temperature. After carefully adding the scallops, brown them for two mins on every end. The scallops should be served with the blood orange sauce and chives should be used as a topping.

Per servings: Calories: 140kcal; Fat: 4g; Carbs: 12g; Protein: 15g

90. Salmon and Radish Mix

Preparation time: 10 mins

Cooking time: 15 mins

Servings: four

Ingredients:

- two tbsps. olive oil
- one tbsp. balsamic vinegar
- 1 and ½ cup chicken stock
- 4 salmon fillets, boneless
- 2 garlic cloves, minced
- 1 tablespoon ginger, grated
- 1 cup radishes, grated
- ¼ cup scallions, chopped

Directions:

1. Warm up a pot using the oil across moderate-high flame, include the salmon, cook for four mins on every end, and divide between plates

2. Add the vinegar and the rest of the ingredients to the pan, toss gently, cook for 10 minutes, add over the salmon and serve.

Per servings: Calories: 332.9kcal; Fat: 22.3g; Carbs: 6g; Protein: 27g

CHAPTER 6
SALADS & VEGETABLES

91. Steamed Squash Chowder	60
92. Vegetarian Coconut Curry	60
93. Stewed Okra	60
94. Dill Cucumber Salad	61
95. Vegan Sesame Tofu and Eggplants	61
96. Sautéed Kale with Tomato	61
97. Italian White Bean Salad with Bell Peppers	62
98. Cheesy Tomato Salad	62
99. Fennel and Walnuts Salad	62
100. Roasted Golden Beet and Watercress Salad	63
101. Cauliflower Tabbouleh Salad	63
102. Roasted Eggplant and Chickpeas with Tomato Sauce	64
103. Cheesy Potato Mash	64
104. Quick Vegetable Kebabs	65
105. Veggie Lo Mein	65

91. Steamed Squash Chowder

Preparation time: twenty mins

Cooking time: 35-40 mins

Servings: four

Ingredients:

- three cups chicken broth
- two tbsps. ghee
- one teaspoon chili powder
- half teaspoon cumin
- one and a half teaspoon salt
- two tsps. cinnamon
- three tbsps. olive oil
- two carrots, sliced
- one small yellow onion, sliced
- one green apple, cut and cored
- one big butternut squash, skinned, seeded, and sliced into half inch cubes

Directions:

1. Within a big griddle set across moderate-high flame, melt the butter until it is completely dissolved. Fry the onions in the heated ghee for five mins, or till they are tender and translucent, whichever comes first.

2. Mix in the chilli powder, cumin, salt, and cinnamon with the olive oil and chilli powder. Fry for 1/2 min.

3. After adding the zucchini and apples in sliced form, continue to fry the mixture for ten mins, mixing occasionally.

4. Once the apples and zucchini have reached the desired tenderness, include the broth, cover, and continue cooking across moderate flame for another twenty mins.

5. Puree the chowder using an immersion blender. Serve and enjoy.

Per servings: Calories: 228kcal; Fat: 18g; Carbs: 17g; Protein: 2g

92. Vegetarian Coconut Curry

Preparation time: 10 minutes

Cooking time: 10-15 minutes

Servings: 4

Ingredients:

- 4 tbsp coconut oil
- 1 medium onion, chopped
- 1 tsp minced garlic
- 1 tsp minced ginger
- 1 cup broccoli florets
- 2 cups fresh spinach leaves
- 2 tsp fish sauce
- 1 tbsp garam masala
- ½ cup coconut milk
- Salt & pepper, as required

Directions:

1. Warm the oil in your pot across moderate flame. Sauté the onion and garlic for 3 mins until fragrant.

2. Except for the spinach leaves, stir in the other ingredients. Top using salt and pepper as required.

3. Cover and cook over medium flame for 5 mins.

4. Stir well, add the spinach leaves, cover, and cook for 2 minutes. Let it sit for two more mins prior to offering.

Per servings: Calories: 210kcal; Fat: 20g; Carbs: 6g; Protein: 2g

93. Stewed Okra

Preparation time: ten mins

Cooking time: 19-20 mins

Servings: four

Ingredients:

- quarter cup extra-virgin olive oil

- one large onion, sliced
- 4 cloves garlic, finely chopped
- 1 tsp salt
- 1 pound fresh or frozen okra, cleaned
- 1 (15-oz) can of plain tomato sauce
- 2 cups water
- ½ cup fresh cilantro, finely chopped
- ½ tsp freshly ground black pepper

Directions:

1. Cook the onion, garlic, and salt in the olive oil within a large saucepan across moderate flame while stirring frequently for one min. After stirring it in, simmer the okra for three mins.

2. After mixing in the tomato sauce, water, cilantro, and black pepper, conceal the pot, and continue cooking over medium heat for fifteen mins, swirling a few times during that time. To be served hot.

Per servings: Calories: 201kcal; Fat: 14g; Carbs: 18g; Protein: 4g

94. Dill Cucumber Salad

Preparation time: ten mins
Cooking time: 0 mins
Servings: 8
Ingredients:

- four cucumbers, sliced
- one cup white wine vinegar
- two white onions, cut
- 1 tbsp dill, sliced

Directions:

1. Combine the cucumber via the onions, vinegar, and dill in a bowl.

2. Store in the refrigerator for one hr prior to offering as a side salad.

Per servings: Calories: 182kcal; Fat: 3g; Carbs: 8g; Protein: 4g

95. Vegan Sesame Tofu and Eggplants

Preparation time: ten mins
Cooking time: 16-20 mins
Servings: four
Ingredients:

- 5 tbsps. olive oil
- one pound firm tofu, sliced
- 3 tbsp rice vinegar
- 2 tsp Swerve sweetener
- 2 whole eggplants, sliced
- ¼ cup soy sauce
- Salt & pepper, as required
- 4 tbsp toasted sesame oil
- ¼ cup sesame seeds
- 1 cup fresh cilantro, chopped

Directions:

1. Warm a pot using oil across moderate flame and cook the tofu for 3 mins on every end.

2. Stir in the rice vinegar, sweetener, eggplants, and soy sauce. Flavor it with salt and pepper.

3. Cover and cook 5 minutes over medium heat. Cook for another 5 minutes, stirring constantly.

4. Add the rest of the fixings, and toss thoroughly. Offer and relish.

Per servings: Calories: 513kcal; Fat: 49.2g; Carbs: 19g; Protein: 23.9g

96. Sautéed Kale with Tomato

Preparation time: ten mins
Cooking time: ten mins
Servings: four
Ingredients:

- 1 tablespoon extra-virgin olive oil
- 4 garlic cloves, sliced
- ¼ tsp red pepper flakes

- 2 bunches kale, stemmed & chopped
- one (fourteen and a half oz) can of no-salt-included chopped tomatoes
- ½ tsp kosher salt

Directions:

1. Warm the olive oil in your big griddle across moderate-high flame. Include the garlic and red pepper flakes then fry for 30 seconds till fragrant.

2. Add the kale and sauté for three to five mins, till the kale shrinks mildly. Include the tomatoes and the salt then stir well.

3. Cook 3 to 5 minutes or until the liquid reduces. Serve.

Per servings: Calories: 110kcal; Fat: 5g; Carbs: 15g; Protein: 6g

97. Italian White Bean Salad with Bell Peppers

Preparation time: fifteen mins
Cooking time: 0 mins
Servings: four
Ingredients:

- two tbsp additional-virgin olive oil
- two tbsp white wine vinegar
- ½ shallot, minced
- ½ teaspoon kosher salt
- ¼ teaspoon freshly ground black pepper
- 3 cups cooked cannellini beans, drained & rinsed
- 2 celery stalks, diced
- ½ red bell pepper, diced
- ¼ cup fresh parsley, sliced
- ¼ cup fresh mint, sliced

Directions:

1. Whisk the oil, vinegar, shallot, salt, and black pepper inside a big container.

2. Include the beans, celery, red bell pepper, parsley, and mint; mix thoroughly.

Per servings: Calories: 300kcal; Fat: 8g; Carbs: 46g; Protein: 15g

98. Cheesy Tomato Salad

Preparation time: 5 minutes
Cooking time: 0 minutes
Servings: 4
Ingredients:

- 2 pounds tomatoes, sliced
- 1 red onion, chopped
- 4 oz feta cheese, crumbled
- 2 tbsp mint, chopped
- A drizzle of olive oil
- Sea salt & black pepper, as required

Directions:

1. Mix the entire fixings in your large container and serve.

Per servings: Calories: 190kcal; Fat: 4g; Carbs: 8g; Protein: 3g

99. Fennel and Walnuts Salad

Preparation time: five mins
Cooking time: zero mins
Servings: four
Ingredients:

- 8 dates, pitted & cut
- 2 fennel bulbs, sliced
- 2 tbsp chives, chopped
- ½ cup walnuts, chopped
- 2 tbsp lime juice
- 2 tbsp olive oil
- Salt & black pepper to taste

Directions:

2. In a salad bowl, combine the fennel with dates and the rest of the ingredients. Serve!

Per servings: Calories: 200kcal; Fat: 7g; Carbs: 14g; Protein: 4g

100. Roasted Golden Beet and Watercress Salad

Preparation time: 15 mins

Cooking time: 60 mins

Servings: 4

Ingredients:

- one bunch (about one and a half pounds) golden beets
- one tablespoon extra-virgin olive oil
- 1 tbsp white wine vinegar
- ½ tsp kosher salt
- ¼ tsp freshly ground black pepper
- 1 (about 4 oz) bunch of watercress
- 1 avocado, peeled, pitted, and diced
- ¼ cup crumbled feta cheese
- ¼ cup walnuts, toasted
- 1 tbsp fresh chives, chopped

Directions:

1. Warm up the microwave to 425 deg. F.

2. Wash and trim the beets (cut an inch above the beetroot, leaving the long tail if desired), then wrap each beet individually in foil.

3. Arrange the beets on your baking sheet and roast for 45-60 mins till fully cooked.

4. Eliminate the beets and let them cool. Under cold running water, slough off the skin. Cut the beets into bite-size cubes or wedges.

5. Whisk the oil, vinegar, salt, and black pepper inside a big container. Include the watercress and beets and combine well. Add the avocado, feta, walnuts, and chives and mix gently.

Per servings: Calories: 235kcal; Fat: 16g; Carbs: 21g; Protein: 6g

101. Cauliflower Tabbouleh Salad

Preparation time: fifteen mins

Cooking time: zero mins

Servings: four

Ingredients:

- ¼ cup additional-virgin olive oil
- ¼ cup lemon juice
- Zest of 1 lemon
- ¾ tsp kosher salt
- ½ tsp ground turmeric
- ¼ tsp ground coriander
- ¼ tsp ground cumin
- ¼ tsp black pepper
- one-eighth teaspoon ground cinnamon
- one pound riced cauliflower
- 1 English cucumber, diced
- 12 cherry tomatoes, halved
- 1 cup fresh parsley, sliced
- half cup fresh mint, sliced

Directions:

1. Whisk the olive oil, lemon juice, lemon zest, salt, turmeric, coriander, cumin, black pepper, and cinnamon in a large bowl.

2. Add the cauliflower rice and mix well. Add the cucumber, tomatoes, parsley, and mint and gently mix.

Per servings: Calories: 180kcal; Fat: 15g; Carbs: 12g; Protein: 4g

102. Roasted Eggplant and Chickpeas with Tomato Sauce

Preparation time: fifteen mins

Cooking time: one hr & 15 minutes

Servings: four

Ingredients:

- 1 (around one lb.) large eggplant, cut into quarter inch dense rounds
- one tsp kosher salt, split
- one tbsp additional-virgin olive oil
- three garlic cloves, crushed
- one (twenty-eight oz) can of no-salt-included crumpled tomatoes
- ½ tsp honey
- ¼ tsp freshly ground black pepper
- two tbsp fresh basil, sliced
- one (fifteen-oz) can of no-salt-included or low-sodium chickpeas, wearied and washed
- three-quarter cup crumbled feta cheese
- one tbsp fresh oregano, sliced
- Olive oil cooking spray

Directions:

1. Assemble two baking dishes by lining them with foil and greasing them via cooking spray before preheating the microwave to 425 degrees Fahrenheit.

2. Drizzle a half tsp. of salt over the eggplant after it has been arranged in a uniform layer. Bake for twenty mins, turning briefly till the vegetables are golden brown.

3. Although that is happening, bring the olive oil to a simmer in the big pot you have. After adding the garlic and continuing to fry for another forty secs.

4. Next, stir in the honey, the extra half tsp. of salt, and some freshly ground black pepper. Simmer for about twenty mins, or till the sauce reaches the desired consistency. Mix in the chopped cilantro.

5. Once taking the eggplant out of the microwave, lower the temp. to 375 degrees Fahrenheit and keep the microwave on.

6. Place the chickpeas and one cup of the sauce in a big baking dish that is either rectangular or circular in shape. On surface of the chickpeas, layer the sliced eggplant so that they overhang and conceal everything.

7. Spread and distribute the rest of the sauce across the surface in a uniform layer. The feta cheese and the rosemary should be sprinkled on top.

8. Prepare the baking tray with foil, then place it in the oven for fifteen mins. Take off the paper, and continue baking for another fifteen mins.

Per servings: Calories: 320kcal; Fat: 11g; Carbs: 40g; Protein: 14g

103. Cheesy Potato Mash

Preparation time: 10 minutes

Cooking time: 20 minutes

Servings: 8

Ingredients:

- 2 pounds gold potatoes, peeled and cubed
- 1 ½ cup cream cheese, soft
- Sea salt & black pepper to taste
- ½ cup almond milk
- 2 tbsp chives, chopped

Directions:

1. Place potatoes in a pot, add water to cover and a pinch of salt. Let it boil across moderate flame, and cook for 20 mins. Drain well and mash them.

2. Include the rest of the components, excluding for the chives, and whisk thoroughly. Include the chives, stir well, and serve.

Per servings: Calories: 243kcal; Fat: 6g; Carbs: 5g; Protein: 5g

104. Quick Vegetable Kebabs

Preparation time: fifteen mins

Cooking time: 10 mins

Servings: six

Ingredients:

- 4 average red onions, skinned and cut into 6 wedges
- 4 medium zucchinis, sliced into 1-inch-thick slices
- 4 bell peppers sliced into 2-inch squares
- 2 yellow bell peppers, sliced into 2-inch squares
- 2 orange bell peppers, sliced into 2-inch squares
- 2 beefsteak tomatoes, sliced into quarters
- 3 tbsp herbed oil

Directions:

1. The microwave should be preheated to 350 deg. F.
2. Thread 1-piece red onion, zucchini, different colored bell peppers, and tomatoes onto a skewer.
3. Repeat until the skewer is full of vegetables, up to 2 inches from the skewer end, and continue until all skewers are complete.
4. Put the skewers on your baking sheet and cook in your microwave for 10 mins. The vegetables will be done with they reach your desired crunchiness or softness.
5. Remove the skewers from the heat and drizzle with herbed oil.

Per servings: Calories: 235kcal; Fat: 14g; Carbs: 30g; Protein: 8g

105. Veggie Lo Mein

Preparation time: 10 minutes

Cooking time: 4 minutes

Servings: 6

Ingredients:

- 2 tbsp olive oil
- 5 cloves of garlic, minced
- 2-inch knob of ginger, grated
- 8 oz mushrooms, sliced
- ½ pound zucchini, spiralized
- 1 carrot, julienned
- 1 green spring onions, chopped
- 3 tbsp coconut aminos
- Salt & pepper, as required
- one tbsp sesame oil

Directions:

1. Warm the oil in a skillet and sauté the garlic and ginger until fragrant. Stir in the mushrooms, zucchini, carrot, and green onions.
2. Season with coconut aminos, salt, and pepper. Conceal the cover and permit it to low boil for five mins. Drizzle using sesame oil and serve.

Per servings: Calories: 288kcal; Fat: 11g; Carbs: 48.7g; Protein: 7.6g

CHAPTER 7
SNACKS & APPETIZERS

106. Spicy Watermelon Mango Salsa	67
107. Stuffed Avocado	67
108. Loukoumades (Fried Honey Balls)	67
109. Feta Artichoke Dip	68
110. Tomato Bruschetta	68
111. Watermelon And Blueberry Salad	68
112. Cannellini Romesco Dip	69
113. Cucumber Hummus Bites	69
114. Dried Fruit Compote	69
115. Vinegar Beet Bites	70
116. Prosciutto Wrapped Plums	70
117. Lentils and Cheddar Frittata	70
118. Tomato Salsa	70
119. Salmon Rolls	71
120. Pumpkin-Spiced Quinoa	71

106. Spicy Watermelon Mango Salsa

Preparation time: 10 minutes

Cooking time: 0 minutes

Servings: 3

Ingredients:

- 1/2 cup seedless, peeled & cubed watermelon
- 1 peeled & chopped mango
- 1 red tomato, chopped
- 1 sliced red onion
- 1 sliced chili pepper
- one-eighth cup chopped cilantro
- 1 1/2 tbsps. lime juice
- Salt & black pepper, as required

Directions:

1. Combine the tomato with the watermelon, onion, and remaining components, excluding for the pita chips, in a container.

2. Divide the mixture into small cups and serve.

Per servings: Calories: 62kcal; Fat: 4g; Carbs: 3g; Protein: 2g

107. Stuffed Avocado

Preparation time: ten mins

Cooking time: zero mins

Servings: two

Ingredients:

- 1 avocado, halved & pitted
- 10 oz canned tuna, drained
- 2 tbsp sun-dried tomatoes, chopped
- 1 ½ tbsp basil pesto
- 2 tbsp black olives, pitted & chopped
- Salt & black pepper to taste
- 2 tsp pine nuts, toasted & chopped
- 1 tbsp basil, chopped

Directions:

1. Combine the tuna and the rest of the components, excluding for the avocado, inside a container.

2. Stuff this mixture in each avocado half and serve.

Per servings: Calories: 233kcal; Fat: 9g; Carbs: 11g; Protein: 5g

108. Loukoumades (Fried Honey Balls)

Preparation time: 20 minutes

Cooking time: 45 minutes

Servings: 10

Ingredients:

- 2 cups sugar
- 1 cup water
- 1 cup honey
- 1 ½ cup tepid water
- 1 tablespoon brown sugar
- ¼ cup vegetable oil
- one tbsp. lively dry yeast
- one and a half cups all-purpose flour, 1 cup cornstarch, ½ teaspoon salt
- Vegetable oil for frying
- one and a half cup sliced walnuts
- ¼ cup ground cinnamon

Directions:

1. Boil the sugar & water on moderate flame. Include honey after 10 minutes. Cool and set aside.

2. Mix the tepid water, oil, brown sugar,' and yeast in a large bowl. Allow it to sit for 10 minutes. Inside a distinct container, mix the flour, salt, and cornstarch. Mix the yeast and flour with your hands to make a wet dough. Conceal and cast away for 2 hours.

3. Fry in oil at 350 deg. F. Use your palm to measure the sizes of the pieces of dough as they are dropped into the frying pan. Fry each batch for about 3-4 minutes.

4. Immediately after the loukoumades are done frying, drop them in the prepared syrup.

5. Serve with cinnamon and walnuts.

Per servings: Calories: 355kcal; Fat: 7g; Carbs: 64g; Protein: 6g

109. Feta Artichoke Dip

Preparation time: ten mins

Cooking time: thirty mins

Servings: eight

Ingredients:

- eight oz canned artichoke hearts, drained & quartered
- ¾ cup basil, chopped
- ¾ cup green olives, pitted & chopped
- 1 cup parmesan cheese, grated
- 5 oz feta cheese, crumbled

Directions:

1. In your food processor, pulse the artichokes and the remaining ingredients.

2. Transfer to a baking dish, bake in the oven at 375 deg. F for 30 minutes, and serve as a party dip.

Per servings: Calories: 186kcal; Fat: 12g; Carbs: 2g; Protein: 1g

110. Tomato Bruschetta

Preparation time: 10 mins

Cooking time: zero mins

Servings: 2

Ingredients:

- 4 oz halved cherry tomatoes
- 1/4 cup fresh herbs, chopped
- 1/8 cup ricotta cheese
- half tablespoon additional-virgin olive oil
- one-eighth teaspoon each of kosher salt & freshly ground black pepper
- 2 slices of toasted whole-wheat bread

Directions:

1. Within a moderate dish, mix the tomato, herb, and olive oil mixture along with the salt and black pepper.

2. Ricotta cheese should be evenly distributed across each piece of bread. Within every piece of bruschetta, evenly distribute one-fourth of the tomato combination. To garnish with additional herbs, do so if preferred.

Per servings: Calories: 100kcal; Fat: 6g; Carbs: 10g; Protein: 4g

111. Watermelon And Blueberry Salad

Preparation time: five mins

Cooking time: 0 mins

Servings: 6 to 8

Ingredients:

- one medium watermelon
- one cup fresh blueberries
- ⅓ cup honey
- 2 tablespoons lemon juice
- 2 tablespoons finely chopped fresh mint leaves

Directions:

1. Cut the watermelon into 1-inch cubes. Put them in a bowl.

2. Evenly distribute the blueberries over the watermelon.

3. Beat simultaneously the honey, lemon juice, and mint inside a separate container. Drizzle the mint dressing over the watermelon and blueberries. Serve cold.

Per servings: Calories: 238kcal; Fat: 1.0g; Carbs: 61.0g; Protein: 4.0g

112. Cannellini Romesco Dip

Preparation time: 15 mins

Cooking time: zero mins

Servings: two cups

Ingredients:

- half (7 oz) can of no-salt-added diced tomatoes
- 1/2 (7 oz) can of low-sodium cannellini beans, wearied and washed
- half (6-oz) jar of roasted sweet red peppers in water, drained
- quarter cup roasted unsalted almonds
- 1 (3-inch) multigrain pita, torn into small parts
- one garlic clove, peeled
- one-eighth cup additional-virgin olive oil
- one tablespoon red wine vinegar
- half tablespoon fresh parsley, chopped
- half teaspoon red pepper flakes
- half teaspoon each of sweet or smoked paprika & kosher salt
- 1/8 tsp black pepper

Directions:

1. Pulse the garlic in your mixing bowl until minced. Include the almonds, pita, and red pepper flakes and process until minced.
2. Combine the sweet red peppers, tomatoes, beans, parsley, paprika, salt, and black pepper in a mixing bowl. Blend until smooth.
3. While your processor is running, add the olive oil and vinegar then process until smooth. Serve!

Per servings: Calories: 180kcal; Fat: 10g; Carbs: 20g; Protein: 6g

113. Cucumber Hummus Bites

Preparation time: 15 mins

Cooking time: zero mins

Servings: 6 bites

Ingredients:

- half English cucumber, cut
- 3 cherry tomatoes, halved
- 5 oz hummus
- 1/2 oz feta cheese, crumbled
- 1/2 tbsp parsley, chopped

Directions:

1. Disperse the hummus on every cucumber and split the tomato halves on every.
2. Drizzle the cheese and parsley onto it and offer as a sample.

Per servings: Calories: 162kcal; Fat: 3g; Carbs: 6g; Protein: 2g

114. Dried Fruit Compote

Preparation time: 5 minutes

Cooking time: 20 minutes

Servings: 6

Ingredients:

- 8 oz dried apricots, quartered
- 8 oz dried peaches, quartered
- one cup golden raisins
- one and a half cup orange juice
- one cinnamon stick
- 4 whole cloves

Directions:

1. Stir to merge. Close, select the Manual button, and adjust the time to 3 mins. Once the timer beeps, let the pressure release naturally for about 20 mins. Press the Cancel button, then open the lid.
2. Remove and discard the cinnamon and cloves.
3. Press the Sauté button and simmer for 5–6 minutes. Serve warm, then cover and refrigerate for up to a week.

Per servings: Calories: 258kcal; Fat: 5g; Carbs: 8g; Protein: 4g

115. Vinegar Beet Bites

Preparation time: ten mins

Cooking time: 30 mins

Servings: 4

Ingredients:

- 2 beets, sliced
- A pinch of sea salt & black pepper
- one-third cup balsamic vinegar
- one cup olive oil

Directions:

1. Spread the beet pieces on your baking sheet lined using parchment paper.

2. Add the remaining components, whisk, and bake at 350 deg. F for thirty mins. Serve the beet bites cold as a snack.

Per servings: Calories: 199kcal; Fat: 5g; Carbs: 8g; Protein: 3g

116. Prosciutto Wrapped Plums

Preparation time: five mins

Cooking time: 0 mins

Servings: two

Ingredients:

- two plums, quartered
- 1 oz prosciutto, cut into 8 pieces
- 1/2 tbsp chives, chopped
- red pepper flakes to taste, crumpled

Directions:

1. Embed every plum portion with a prosciutto piece.

2. Sprinkle it with chives and pepper flakes before serving.

Per servings: Calories: 30kcal; Fat: 1g; Carbs: 4g; Protein: 2g

117. Lentils and Cheddar Frittata

Preparation time: ten mins

Cooking time: fifteen mins

Servings: four

Ingredients:

- one red onion, sliced
- 2 tbsp olive oil
- 1 cup sweet potatoes, boiled and chopped
- 4 eggs, whisked
- ¾ cup lentils, cooked
- 2 tbsp Greek yogurt
- Salt & black pepper, as required
- half cup cherry tomatoes shared
- ¾ cup cheddar cheese, grated

Directions:

1. Warm up a pot using the oil across moderate flame and sauté the onion for 2 mins.

2. Include the sweet potatoes, lentils, yogurt, cherry tomatoes, salt, and pepper then cook for additional three mins.

3. Include the whisked eggs, and cheese, cover, and cook ten mins.

4. Slice the frittata, divide among plates, and offer.

Per servings: Calories: 200kcal; Fat: 15g; Carbs: 3g; Protein: 12g

118. Tomato Salsa

Preparation time: 5 mins

Cooking time: 0 mins

Servings: 6

Ingredients:

- one garlic clove, minced
- 4 tbsp olive oil
- 5 tomatoes, cubed
- 1 tbsp balsamic vinegar

- ¼ cup basil, chopped
- 1 tbsp parsley, chopped
- 1 tbsp chives, chopped
- Salt & black pepper to taste
- Pita chips for serving

Directions:

1. Within a dish, combine all of the components, with the exception of the pita chips: tomatoes, garlic, and the other components.

2. For serving, split the mixture into individual cups, and pass the pita pieces on along with it.

Per servings: Calories: 160kcal; Fat: 13g; Carbs: 10g; Protein: 2g

119. Salmon Rolls

Preparation time: 5 minutes
Cooking time: 0 minutes
Servings: 12 rolls
Ingredients:

- 1 large & long cucumber, thinly sliced lengthwise
- 2 tsp lime juice
- 4 oz cream cheese, soft
- 1 tsp lemon zest, grated
- Salt & black pepper to taste
- 2 tsp dill, chopped
- 4 oz smoked salmon, cut into strips

Directions:

1. Arrange cucumber slices on a working surface and top each with a salmon strip.

2. In your bowl, mix the remaining ingredients, stir, and spread over the salmon.

3. Roll the salmon and cucumber strips, arrange them on your serving plate, and serve.

Per servings: Calories: 245kcal; Fat: 15g; Carbs: 16g; Protein: 17g

120. Pumpkin-Spiced Quinoa

Preparation time: 10 minutes
Cooking time: 20-25 minutes
Servings: 4
Ingredients:

- 1/2 cup quinoa, rinsed
- 3/4 cup steel-cut oats
- 1/4 tsp kosher salt
- 3 cups water
- 3 tbsp raw honey
- 1 tsp pumpkin pie spice
- 3/4 cup canned pumpkin
- one-third cup lightly toasted walnuts, roughly sliced
- half cup dried cranberries
- A splash of almond milk

Directions:

1. Bring the water, salt, oats, and quinoa to a boil in a pot across moderate flame.

2. Adjust to a low boil and cook for 20 mins, covered. Stir in the canned pumpkin, pumpkin spice, and honey.

3. Let the pot stand covered for 5 mins till the entire liquids are riveted and the quinoa and oats have softened.

4. Gently stir in the walnuts and dried cranberries. Serve with a few splashes of almond milk, if desired.

Per servings: Calories: 361kcal; Fat: 10g; Carbs: 65g; Protein: 9g

CHAPTER 8
JUICE & SMOOTHIES

121. Kale-Pineapple Smoothie	73
122. Hearty Pear and Mango Smoothie	73
123. Honey And Wild Blueberry Smoothie	73
124. Oats Berry Smoothie	73
125. Fruit Smoothie	74
126. Blueberry Banana; Protein: Smoothie	74
127. Moroccan Avocado Smoothie	74
128. Cranberry-Pumpkin Smoothie	74
129. Peanut Butter Banana Greek Yogurt	75
130. Avocado-Blueberry Smoothie	75
131. Raspberry Vanilla Smoothie	75
132. Almond Butter Banana Chocolate Smoothie	75
133. Mango-Pear Smoothie	76
134. Mediterranean Smoothie	76
135. Chia-Pomegranate Smoothie	76

121. Kale-Pineapple Smoothie

Preparation time: five mins

Cooking time: 5 mins

Servings: two

Ingredients:

- 1 Persian cucumber
- fresh mint
- one cup of coconut milk
- 1 tablespoon honey
- one and a half cups of pineapple pieces
- ¼ pound baby kale

Directions:

1. Cut the ends off of the cucumbers and then cut the whole cucumber into small cubes. Strip the mint leaves from the stems.

2. Include the entire components to your instant pan Ace blender and blend until smooth.

Per servings: Calories: 421.5kcal; Fat: 29g; Carbs: 44g; Protein: 5.12g

122. Hearty Pear and Mango Smoothie

Preparation time: 10 minutes

Cooking time: nil

Servings: 1

Ingredients:

- 1 ripe mango, cored and chopped
- ½ mango, peeled, pitted, and chopped
- 1 cup kale, chopped
- ½ cup plain Greek yogurt
- 2 ice cubes

Directions:

1. Include pear, mango, yogurt, kale, and mango to a mixer and puree.

2. Add ice and blend until you have a smooth texture.

3. Serve and enjoy!

Per servings: Calories: 361kcal; Fat: 8.1g; Carbs: 62.6g; Protein: 16.8g

123. Honey And Wild Blueberry Smoothie

Preparation time: five mins

Cooking time: ten mins

Servings: two

Ingredients:

- one whole banana
- 1 cup mango chunks
- ½ cup wild blueberries
- ½ plain, nonfat Greek yogurt
- ½ cup milk (for blending)
- 1 tablespoon raw honey
- ½ cup of kale

Directions:

1. Include the entire components into an instant pan Ace blender. Add extra ice cubes if needed.

2. Process until smooth.

Per servings: Calories: 207kcal; Fat: 2.69g; Carbs: 42.56g; Protein: 7g

124. Oats Berry Smoothie

Preparation time: five mins

Cooking time: 5 mins

Servings: two

Ingredients:

- 1 cup frozen berries
- one cup Greek yogurt
- ¼ cup milk
- ¼ cup oats
- 2 teaspoon honey

Directions:

1. Place all Ingredients in an instant pot Ace blender and blend until smooth.

Per servings: Calories: 247kcal; Fat: 7.6g; Carbs: 32.8g; Protein: 13.9g

125. Fruit Smoothie

Preparation time: five mins

Cooking time: zero mins

Servings: two

Ingredients:

- two cups blueberries (or any fresh or frozen fruit, cut into pieces if the fruit is large)
- two cups unsweetened almond milk
- one cup crushed ice
- ½ tsp. ground ginger (or other dried ground spice such as turmeric, cinnamon, or nutmeg)

Directions:

1. Inside a mixer, blend the blueberries, almond milk, ice, and ginger. Mix till uniform.

Per servings: Calories: 125kcal; Fat: 3.3g; Carbs: 23.3g; Protein: 2.68g

126. Blueberry Banana; Protein: Smoothie

Preparation time: 5 minutes

Cooking time: 5 minutes

Servings: 1

Ingredients:

- ½ cup frozen and unsweetened blueberries
- ½ banana slices up
- ¾ cup plain nonfat Greek yogurt
- ¾ cup unsweetened vanilla almond milk
- 2 cups of ice cubes

Directions:

1. Include the entire components into an instant pan ace blender.
2. Blend until smooth.

Per servings: Calories: 202kcal; Fat: 3.15g; Carbs: 29g; Protein: 17g

127. Moroccan Avocado Smoothie

Preparation time: 5 mins

Cooking time: zero mins

Servings: 4

Ingredients:

- one ripe avocado, peeled and eroded
- one overripe banana
- 1 cup almond milk, unsweetened
- 1 cup of ice

Directions:

1. Place the avocado, banana, milk, and ice into your instant pot Ace blender.
2. Blend until smooth with no pieces of avocado remaining.

Per servings: Calories: 80.48kcal; Fat: 4.89g; Carbs: 9.48g; Protein: 1.2g

128. Cranberry-Pumpkin Smoothie

Preparation time: five mins

Cooking time: 0 mins

Servings: two

Ingredients:

- 2 cups unsweetened almond milk
- one cup pure pumpkin purée
- ¼ cup gluten-free rolled oats
- ¼ cup pure cranberry juice (no sugar added)
- 1 tablespoon honey
- ¼ tsp. ground cinnamon
- tweak of ground nutmeg

Directions:

1. In a blender, combine the almond milk, pumpkin, oats, cranberry juice, honey, cinnamon, and nutmeg and mix till uniform.
2. Put into glasses and offer immediately.

Per servings: Calories: 175kcal; Fat: 3.7g; Carbs: 32.8g; Protein: 4.3g

129. Peanut Butter Banana Greek Yogurt

Preparation time: ten mins

Cooking time: 30-40 seconds

Servings: four

Ingredients:

- 3 cups vanilla Greek yogurt
- two average bananas cut
- quarter cup creamy natural peanut butter
- ¼ cup flaxseed meal
- 1 tsp nutmeg

Directions:

1. Divide yogurt between four jars with lids. Top with banana slices.

2. In a container, dissolve the peanut butter inside an oven-safe bowl for 60 secs. Sprinkle peanut butter on each jar and let it chill in your fridge before serving.

3. When ready to serve, sprinkle with a flaxseed meal and ground nutmeg. Enjoy!

Per servings: Calories: 370kcal; Fat: 10g; Carbs: 47g; Protein: 22g

130. Avocado-Blueberry Smoothie

Preparation time: five mins

Cooking time: 0 mins

Servings: two

Ingredients:

- half cup unsweetened vanilla almond milk
- 4 ice cubes
- ½ cup low-fat plain Greek yogurt
- ½ teaspoon vanilla extract
- 1 ripe avocado, peeled, pitted, and coarsely chopped
- 1 cup blueberries
- ¼ cup gluten-free rolled oats

Directions:

1. In a blender, combine the almond milk, yogurt, avocado, blueberries, oats, and vanilla and pulse until well blended.

2. Add the ice cubes and blend till dense and uniform. Distribute.

Per servings: Calories: 188.9kcal; Fat: 10.3g; Carbs: 27g; Protein: 6g

131. Raspberry Vanilla Smoothie

Preparation time: five mins

Cooking time: 5 mins

Servings: over two cups

Ingredients:

- 1 cup frozen raspberries
- 6-ounce container of vanilla Greek yogurt
- ½ cup of unsweetened vanilla almond milk

Directions:

1. Take all of your Ingredients and place them in an instant pot Ace blender.

2. Process until smooth and liquified.

Per servings: Calories: 143.9kcal; Fat: 5.68g; Carbs: 16.47g; Protein: 8g

132. Almond Butter Banana Chocolate Smoothie

Preparation time: five mins

Cooking time: 30 mins

Servings: two

Ingredients:

- three-quarter cup almond milk
- half average banana, preferably frozen
- ¼ cup frozen blueberries
- one tbsp. almond butter

- one tbsp. unsweetened cocoa powder
- one tablespoon chia seeds

Directions:

1. Inside a mixer or Vitamix, add the entire components. Mix to combine.

2. Peanut butter, sunflower seed butter, and other kinds of nut butter are good choices to replace the almond butter

Per servings: Calories: 125kcal; Fat: 9g; Carbs: 8g; Protein: 2g

133. Mango-Pear Smoothie

Preparation time: ten mins

Cooking time: zero mins

Servings: one

Ingredients:

- one ripe pear, cored & sliced
- ½ mango, peeled, pitted, and chopped
- 1 cup chopped kale
- ½ cup plain Greek yogurt
- 2 ice cubes

Directions:

1. In a blender, purée the pear, mango, kale, and yogurt.

2. Add the ice and blend until thick and smooth. Pour the smoothie into a glass then serve cold.

Per servings: Calories: 299kcal; Fat: 7.47g; Carbs: 48.5g; Protein: 15.4g

134. Mediterranean Smoothie

Preparation time: 5 minutes

Cooking time: 5 minutes

Servings: 2

Ingredients:

- 2 cups of baby spinach
- 1 teaspoon fresh ginger root
- 1 frozen banana, pre-sliced
- 1 small mango
- ½ cup beet juice
- ½ cup of skim milk
- 4-6 ice cubes

Directions:

1. Take all Ingredients and place them in your instant pot Ace blender.

Per servings: Calories: 148.7kcal; Fat: 0.77g; Carbs: 33.56g; Protein: 4.8g

135. Chia-Pomegranate Smoothie

Preparation time: five mins

Cooking time: zero mins

Servings: two

Ingredients:

- one cup pure pomegranate juice (no sugar included)
- one cup frozen berries
- one cup coarsely chopped kale
- 2 tablespoons chia seeds
- 3 Medjool dates, pitted and coarsely chopped
- Pinch ground cinnamon

Directions:

1. In a blender, combine the pomegranate juice, berries, kale, chia seeds, dates, and cinnamon and pulse till homogenous. Put into glasses and offer.

Per servings: Calories: 238.47kcal; Fat: 4.67g; Carbs: 49.8g; Protein: 4.5g

CHAPTER 9
DESSERTS

136. Easy Strawberry Crepes Recipe	78
137. Easy Roasted Fruit Recipe	78
138. Kourabiedes Almond Cookies	79
139. Mint Banana Chocolate Sorbet	79
140. Mango And Coconut Frozen Pie	79
141. Lemony Blackberry Granita	80
142. Strawberries With Balsamic Vinegar	80
143. Raspberry Yogurt Basted Cantaloupe	80
144. Chocolate And Avocado Mousse	81
145. Apple and Berries Ambrosia	81
146. Crème Caramel	81
147. Pear Croustade	82
148. Frozen Mango Raspberry Delight	82
149. Triple Chocolate Tiramisu	82
150. Revani Syrup Cake	83

136. Easy Strawberry Crepes Recipe

Preparation time: ten mins

Cooking time: 12 mins

Servings: 12

Ingredients:

- two cups sliced frozen strawberries, thawed
- 2 tablespoons sugar
- ½ teaspoon orange zest, optional
- 3 cups fresh strawberries, diced
- 2 large eggs
- 2 tablespoons butter, slightly melted and cooled
- 2 cups milk
- 1 teaspoon vanilla
- 1 tablespoon sugar
- ½ teaspoon salt
- 1 ½ cups flour

Directions:

For the Strawberry filling:

1. Gently puree the strawberries to thaw. Stir in honey, orange zest if using, and fresh sliced strawberries. Serve at room temperature with a strawberry filling.

For Crêpes:

1. In the order listed, add the components to the mixer jar, cover and mix till uniform.

2. Until cooking, refrigerate overnight or for 1 hour. (Or you can strain any lumps and use them immediately if you'd prefer.)

3. Over medium heat, heat the crepe pan or an 8-inch skillet and brush loosely with butter or cooking spray. Pour ¼ cup of batter into the middle of the skillet with each crepe, and then roll the pan so the batter covers the skillet's bottom with a thin layer. Cook for about 1 minute before light brown and the top starts to dry. Flip and boil for an extra 30 seconds.

4. Repeat for the batter that remains. Pile the completed crepes on a tray. (Place wax paper between the crepes if the crepes hold together.) You should put crepes in a 200 degrees C oven to stay warm before they are ready to serve.

5. With a strawberry filling, fill each crepe and roll it up. With whipped cream, serve it.

Per servings: Calories: 120kcal; Fat: 7g; Carbs: 18g; Protein: 6g

137. Easy Roasted Fruit Recipe

Preparation time: 10 minutes

Cooking time: 30 minutes

Servings: 4

Ingredients:

- 4 Peaches, peeled and sliced
- 1 ½ cup Fresh blueberries
- ⅛ teaspoon Ground cinnamon
- 3 tablespoons brown sugar

Directions:

1. Warm up the microwave to 350 deg. F.

2. Within a baking dish, spread the sliced peaches and blueberries. Sprinkled with brown sugar and cinnamon.

3. Bake for about 20 mins at 350 deg. F, then change the oven settings to a low grill and broil for about five min, or until sparkling.

4. Serve warm, cover and refrigerate, or let cool.

Per servings: Calories: 256kcal; Fat: 9g; Carbs: 25g; Protein: 4g

138. Kourabiedes Almond Cookies

Preparation time: 20 minutes

Cooking time: 50 minutes

Servings: 20

Ingredients:

- 1 ½ cups unsalted butter, clarified, at room temperature 2 cups
- 2 cups Confectioners' sugar, divided
- one large egg yolk
- 2 tbsps. brandy
- 1 ½ teaspoon baking powder
- 1 teaspoon vanilla extract
- 5 cups all-purpose flour, sifted
- 1 cup roasted almonds, chopped

Directions:

1. Preheat the oven to 350 deg. F
2. Thoroughly mix butter and ½ cup of sugar in a bowl. Add in the egg after a while. Create a brandy mixture by mixing the brandy and baking powder. Add the mixture to the egg, add vanilla, and then keep beating until the ingredients are properly blended
3. Add flour and almonds to make a dough.
4. Roll the dough to form crescent shapes. You should be able to get about 40 pieces. Put the pieces on a baking sheet, afterwards bake in the microwave for twenty-five mins.
5. Allow the cookies to cool, then coat them with the remaining confectioner's sugar.
6. Serve.

Per servings: Calories: 102kcal; Fat: 7g; Carbs: 10g; Protein: 2g

139. Mint Banana Chocolate Sorbet

Preparation time: four hours 5 mins

Cooking time: zero mins

Servings: 1

Ingredients:

- 1 frozen banana
- one tablespoon almond butter
- two tbsp minced fresh mint
- 2 to 3 tbsp dark chocolate chips (60% cocoa or higher)
- 2 to 3 tbsp goji (optional)

Directions:

1. Place the banana, butter, and mint inside a mixing bowl—beat to purée till creamy and smooth.
2. Add the chocolate and goji, then pulse several more times to mix well. Place the solution into a container or a ramekin, then freeze for around 4 hrs prior to serving chilled.

Per servings: Calories: 213kcal; Fat: 9.8g; Carbs: 2.9g; Protein: 3.1g

140. Mango And Coconut Frozen Pie

Preparation time: 1 hour ten mins

Cooking time: 0 mins

Servings: 8

Ingredients:

Crust:

- one cup cashews
- ½ cup rolled oats
- one cup soft pitted dates
- 1 cup unsweetened coconut milk

Filling:

- 2 large mangoes, peeled and chopped
- ½ cup unsweetened shredded coconut
- ½ cup water

Directions:

1. Combine the crust inside a mixing bowl. Beat to combine thoroughly.

2. Place the solution into an 8-inch springform pan, then press to coat the bottom. Cast away.

3. Combine the filling in the mixing bowl, then beat to purée till smooth.

4. Place the filling across the crust, then utilize a spatula to disperse the filling uniformly. Place the pan in the freeze for 30 mins.

5. Eliminate the pan from the freezer, then allow it to sit for 15 mins under room temperature prior to offering.

Per servings: Calories: 426kcal; Fat: 28.2g; Carbs: 14.9g; Protein: 8.1g

141. Lemony Blackberry Granita

Preparation time: 10 minutes

Cooking time: 0 minutes

Servings: 4

Ingredients:

- 1 pound (454 g) of fresh blackberries
- 1 teaspoon chopped fresh thyme
- ¼ cup freshly squeezed lemon juice
- ½ cup raw honey
- ½ cup water

Directions:

1. Place the rest in a food processor, then beat to purée.

2. Spoon the mixture into a baking dish through a sieve.

3. Discard the seeds that remain in the sieve.

4. Freeze the baking dish for at least 2 hours.

5. Remove the dish from the refrigerator and stir to break any frozen parts.

6. Return the dish to the freezer for an hour, then stir to break any frozen parts again.

7. Return the dish to the freezer for 4 hours until the granita is completely frozen.

8. Remove it from the freezer and mash it to serve.

Per servings: Calories: 183kcal; Fat: 1.1g; Carbs: 45.9g; Protein: 2.2g

142. Strawberries With Balsamic Vinegar

Preparation time: 5 minutes

Cooking time: 0 minutes

Servings: 2

Ingredients:

- 2 cups strawberries, hulled and sliced
- 2 tablespoons sugar
- 2 tbsp balsamic vinegar

Directions:

1. Place the sliced strawberries in a bowl, sprinkle with the sugar, and drizzle with the balsamic vinegar.

2. Toss to combine well and permit it to relax for about ten mins before serving.

Per servings: Calories: 92kcal; Fat: 0.4g; Carbs: 21.7g; Protein: 1.0g

143. Raspberry Yogurt Basted Cantaloupe

Preparation time: 15 minutes

Cooking time: 0 minutes

Servings: 6

Ingredients:

- 2 cups fresh raspberries, mashed
- 1 cup plain coconut yogurt
- ½ teaspoon vanilla extract
- 1 cantaloupe, skinned and cut
- half cup toasted coconut flakes

Directions:

1. Combine the mashed raspberries with yogurt and vanilla extract in a small bowl. Whisk to combine thoroughly.

2. Put the cantaloupe slices on a platter, afterwards top with the raspberry mixture and spread with toasted coconut.

3. Serve immediately.

Per servings: Calories: 75kcal; Fat: 4.1g; Carbs: 10.9g; Protein: 1.2g

144. Chocolate And Avocado Mousse

Preparation time: 40 mins

Cooking time: five mins

Servings: 4 to 6

Ingredients:

- 8 ounces (227 g) dark chocolate (60% cocoa or higher), sliced
- quarter cup unsweetened coconut milk
- two tbsps. coconut oil
- two prepared avocados, deseeded
- ¼ cup raw honey
- Sea salt, as required

Directions:

1. Place the chocolate inside a pot. Place in the coconut milk and afterwards include the coconut oil.

2. Cook for three mins or till the chocolate and coconut oil melt. Stir constantly.

3. Put the avocado in a food processor, then drizzle with honey and melted chocolate. Pulse to combine until smooth.

4. Place the mixture into a serving container, then drizzle with salt. Refrigerate to chill for 30 minutes and serve.

Per servings: Calories: 654kcal; Fat: 46.8g; Carbs: 55.9g; Protein: 7.2g

145. Apple and Berries Ambrosia

Preparation time: 15 minutes

Cooking time: 0 minutes

Servings: 4

Ingredients:

- 2 cups unsweetened coconut milk, chilled
- 2 tablespoons raw honey
- 1 apple, peeled, cored, and chopped
- 2 cups fresh raspberries
- 2 cups fresh blueberries

Directions:

1. Spoon the chilled milk into a big container, then combine in the honey. Stir to combine thoroughly.

2. Then combine in the remaining. Whisk to coat the fruits well and serve them immediately.

Per servings: Calories: 386kcal; Fat: 21.1g; Carbs: 45.9g; Protein: 4.2g

146. Crème Caramel

Preparation time: 60 minutes

Cooking time: 60 minutes

Servings: 12

Ingredients:

- 5 cups whole milk
- 2 teaspoons vanilla extract
- 8 large egg yolks
- 4 large-sized eggs
- 2 cups sugar, divided
- ¼ cup water

Directions:

1. Warm up the microwave to 350 deg. F

2. Heat the milk with medium heat and wait for it to be scalded.

3. Mix 1 cup of sugar and egg yolks in a bowl and add to the eggs.

4. With a nonstick pan on high heat, boil the water and remaining sugar. Do not stir; instead, whirl the pan. When the sugar forms caramel, divide it into ramekins.

5. Place the ramekins in a baking pan and pour the egg mixture into them.

6. Increase water to the pan until it is half full—Bake for thirty mins.

7. Eliminate the ramekins from the baking pan, cool, and then refrigerate for at least 8 hours.

8. Serve.

Per servings: Calories: 110kcal; Fat: 1g; Carbs: 21g; Protein: 2g

147. Pear Croustade

Preparation time: 30 minutes

Cooking time: 60 minutes

Servings: 10

Ingredients:

- 1 cup + 1 tablespoon all-purpose flour, divided
- 4 ½ tablespoons sugar, divided
- ⅛ teaspoon salt
- 6 tablespoons unsalted butter, chilled, cut into ½-inch cubes
- 1 large-sized egg, separated
- 1 ½ tablespoon ice-cold water
- 3 firm, ripe pears (Bosc), peeled, cored, sliced into ¼-inch slices one tbsp. of fresh lemon juice
- one-third tsp. ground allspice
- 1 teaspoon anise seeds

Directions:

1. Pour 1 cup of flour, 1 ½ tablespoon sugar, butter, and salt into a mixing bowl and combine the ingredients by pulsing.

2. Whisk the yolk of the egg and ice water in a separate bowl. Mix the egg solution with the flour mixture. It will produce a dough, wrap it, and cast away for an hr.

3. Set the oven to 400 deg. F.

4. Mix the pear, sugar, leftover flour, allspice, anise seed, and lemon juice inside a big container to make a filling.

5. Arrange the filling in the center of the dough.

6. Bake for about 40 minutes. Cool for about 15 minutes before serving.

Per servings: Calories: 498kcal; Fat: 32g; Carbs: 32g; Protein: 18g

148. Frozen Mango Raspberry Delight

Preparation time: five mins

Cooking time: zero mins

Servings: two

Ingredients:

- 3 cups frozen raspberries
- 1 mango, skinned and rutted
- one peach, skinned and rutted
- 1 teaspoon honey

Directions:

1. Put the entire components inside a mixer and purée, adding water as needed.

2. Put in the freezer for 10 minutes to firm up if desired. Serve chilled or at room temperature.

Per servings: Calories: 276kcal; Fat: 2.1g; Carbs: 60.3g; Protein: 4.5g

149. Triple Chocolate Tiramisu

Preparation time: 10 minutes

Cooking time: 6 hours

Servings: 12

Ingredients:

- 2 3-ounce ladyfingers package, split
- ¼ cup espresso brewed or strong coffee

- 1 8 oz mascarpone carton cheese
- 1 cup whipped cream
- ¼ cup sugar powdered
- 1 teaspoon vanilla
- ⅓ cup chocolate liqueur
- 4 White baking bars of 1 ounce, grated
- 1 oz bittersweet, grated chocolate
- 4 tablespoons Unsweetened cocoa powdered
- Chopped coffee beans covered in chocolate (optional)

Directions:

1. With some ladyfingers, line the bottom of an 8x8x2-inch baking pan, cutting to fit as required. Drizzle over the ladyfingers with half of the espresso; set aside.

2. Beat the mascarpone cheese, powdered sugar, whipped cream, and vanilla with an electric mixer in a medium mixing cup before stiff peaks develop. Up until now, combined, beat in the chocolate liqueur.

3. Spoon half of the mascarpone combination, pouring evenly around the ladyfingers. Sprinkle over the mascarpone mixture of white chocolate and bittersweet chocolate. Top with a different layer of ladyfinger (reserve any leftover ladyfingers for another use)—a layer with the remaining mixture of espresso and mascarpone cheese.

4. For 6 to 24 hours, cover and chill. Sift the cocoa powder over the dessert top. Garnish with cocoa beans, if desired.

5. Make twelve squares.

Per servings: Calories: 256kcal; Fat: 19g; Carbs: 17g; Protein: 6g

150. Revani Syrup Cake

Preparation time: 30 minutes
Cooking time: 3 hours
Servings: 24
Ingredients:

- 1 tablespoon unsalted butter
- 2 tablespoons all-purpose flour
- 1 cup ground rusk or bread crumbs
- 1 cup fine semolina flour
- ¾ cup ground toasted almonds
- 3 teaspoons baking powder
- 16 large eggs
- 2 tablespoons vanilla extract
- 3 cups sugar, divided
- 3 cups water
- 5 (2-inch) strips lemon peel, pith removed
- 3 tablespoons fresh lemon juice
- 1 oz brandy

Directions:

1. Preheat the oven to 350 deg. F, then grease the baking pan with one tablespoon of butter and flour.

2. Combine the rusk, almonds, semolina, and baking powder inside a bowl.

3. In another container, combine the eggs, one cup of sugar, and vanilla; whisk with an electric mixer for about 5 mins. Add the semolina mixture to the eggs and stir.

4. Pour the stirred batter into the greased baking pan and place it in the oven.

5. With the remaining sugar, lemon peels, and water, make the syrup by boiling the mixture on medium heat. Add the lemon juice after 6 minutes, then cook for three mins. Eliminate the lemon peels and cast the syrup away.

6. After the cake is made in the oven, spread the syrup over the cake.

7. Cut the cake as you please and serve.

Per servings: Calories: 348kcal; Fat: 9g; Carbs: 55g; Protein: 5g

Conversion Chart

Volume Equivalents (Liquid)

US Standard	US Standard (ounces)	Metric (approximate)
2 tablespoons	1 fl. oz.	30 mL
¼ cup	2 fl. oz.	60 mL
½ cup	4 fl. oz.	120 mL
1 cup	8 fl. oz.	240 mL
1½ cups	12 fl. oz.	355 mL
2 cups or 1 pint	16 fl. oz.	475 mL
4 cups or 1 quart	32 fl. oz.	1 L
1 gallon	128 fl. oz.	4 L

Volume Equivalents (Dry)

US Standard	Metric (approximate)
⅛ teaspoon	0.5 mL
¼ teaspoon	1 mL
½ teaspoon	2 mL
¾ teaspoon	4 mL
1 teaspoon	5 mL
1 tablespoon	15 mL
¼ cup	59 mL
⅓ cup	79 mL
½ cup	118 mL
⅔ cup	156 mL
¾ cup	177 mL
1 cup	235 mL
2 cups or 1 pint	475 mL
3 cups	700 mL
4 cups or 1 quart	1 L

Oven Temperatures

Fahrenheit (F)	Celsius (C) (approximate)

250°F	120°C
300°F	150°C
325°F	165°C
350°F	180°C
375°F	190°C
400°F	200°C
425°F	220°C
450°F	230°C

Weight Equivalents

US Standard	Metric (approximate)
1 tablespoon	15 g
½ ounce	15 g
1 ounce	30 g
2 ounces	60 g
4 ounces	115 g
8 ounces	225 g
12 ounces	340 g
16 ounces or 1 pound	455 g

12 - Weeks Meal Plan

Week 1

Days	Breakfast	Lunch	Dinner	Dessert	Total Kcal
1	Fruity Breakfast Couscous	Sprouts of Alfalfa and Hummus	Baked Salmon with Garlic Cilantro Sauce	Mint Banana Chocolate Sorbet	1408
2	Fruity Yogurt-Topped Avocado Salad	Mango and Pasta Salad	Fennel and Walnuts Salad	Strawberries with Balsamic Vinegar	766
3	Fig and Ricotta Toast with Walnuts and Honey	Seasoned Beef Kebabs	Greek Lamb Burgers	Chocolate and Avocado Mousse	1699
4	Banana Choco Breakfast Smoothie	Shrimp with White Beans and Feta	Rice and Veggie Jambalaya	Frozen Mango Raspberry Delight	1434
5	Spanish Toasted Tomato Baguettes	Vegan Sesame Tofu and Eggplants	Pecorino Pasta with Sausage and Tomato	Mango and Coconut Frozen Pie	1595
6	Breakfast Quinoa Muffins	Maccheroni With Cherry Tomatoes and Anchovies	Calamari and Dill Sauce	Crème Caramel	991
7	Herb-Encrusted Italian Omelet	Mediterranean Spiced Lentils	Pork Chops and Herbed Tomato Sauce	Triple Chocolate Tiramisu	1052

Week 2

Days	Breakfast	Lunch	Dinner	Dessert	Total Kcal
1	Egg in A "Pepper Hole" With Avocado	Spanish Pepper Steak	Zucchini with Rice and Tzatziki	Easy Strawberry Crepes Recipe	1245
2	Cinnamon Apple and Lentils Porridge	Salmon and Peach Pan	Pork and Herbed Couscous Mix	Kourabiedes Almond Cookies	887.8
3	Harissa Shakshuka With Bell Peppers and Tomatoes	Roasted Eggplant and Chickpeas with Tomato Sauce	Walnut Turkey with Peaches	Raspberry Yogurt Basted Cantaloupe	1085
4	Mediterranean Breakfast Panini	Cucumber Olive Rice	Quick Vegetable Kebabs	Apple and Berries Ambrosia	1271
5	Leeks and Eggs Muffins	Chicken and Bow Tie Pasta	Garlic and Shrimp Pasta	Easy Roasted Fruit Recipe	1232.2
6	Breakfast Yogurt Quinoa	Salmon and Broccoli	Broccoli and Tomato Pasta	Pear Croustade	1404

| 7 | Sun-Dried Tomatoes Oatmeal | Coriander and Coconut Chicken | Spanish Rice Casserole with Cheesy Beef | Lemony Blackberry Granita | 1087 |

Week 3

Days	Breakfast	Lunch	Dinner	Dessert	Total Kcal
1	Apple Quinoa Breakfast Bars	Basil and Sun-Dried Tomatoes Rice	Cinnamon-Glazed Halibut Fillets	Revani Syrup Cake	1313
2	Egg in A "Pepper Hole" With Avocado	Couscous Pudding	Vegetarian Coconut Curry	Easy Roasted Fruit Recipe	936
3	Sun-Dried Tomatoes Oatmeal	Smoked Salmon and Watercress Salad	Greek Turkey Burger	Frozen Mango Raspberry Delight	912.7
4	Cinnamon Apple and Lentils Porridge	Ground Lamb with Lentils and Pomegranate Seeds	Radicchio and Smoked Bacon Risotto	Chocolate and Avocado Mousse	1656
5	Herb-Encrusted Italian Omelet	Italian White Bean Salad with Bell Peppers	Couscous and Apricots Bowls	Easy Strawberry Crepes Recipe	874
6	Fruity Breakfast Couscous	Cinnamon Couscous and Cauliflower	Chopped Tuna Salad	Strawberries with Balsamic Vinegar	990
7	Mediterranean Breakfast Panini	Baked Black-Eyed Peas	Sumac Chicken with Cauliflower and Carrots	Triple Chocolate Tiramisu	1671

Week 4

Days	Breakfast	Lunch	Dinner	Dessert	Total Kcal
1	Fruity Yogurt-Topped Avocado Salad	Crispy Mediterranean Chicken Thighs	Sweet Rice Pudding	Pear Croustade	1807
2	Harissa Shakshuka With Bell Peppers and Tomatoes	White Wine–Sautéed Mussels	Spinach Pesto Pasta	Mango and Coconut Frozen Pie	1606
3	Banana Choco Breakfast Smoothie	Dill Cucumber Salad	Orange Duck and Celery	Mint Banana Chocolate Sorbet	989
4	Spanish Toasted Tomato Baguettes	Bean and Cabbage Soup	Flounder with Tomatoes and Basil	Raspberry Yogurt Basted Cantaloupe	641

5	Fig and Ricotta Toast with Walnuts and Honey	Delicious Chicken Pasta	Seared Scallops with Blood Orange Glaze	Lemony Blackberry Granita	1153
6	Breakfast Quinoa Muffins	Salmon and Radish Mix	Mediterranean Farfalle	Apple and Berries Ambrosia	1533.9
7	Apple Quinoa Breakfast Bars	Pork Tenderloin with Dill Sauce	Baked Mediterranean Rice	Revani Syrup Cake	1109

Week 5

Days	Breakfast	Lunch	Dinner	Dessert	Total Kcal
1	Fruity Breakfast Couscous	Lemon Mushroom Rice	Chicken Shawarma	Mint Banana Chocolate Sorbet	1245
2	Fruity Yogurt-Topped Avocado Salad	Cod and Mushrooms Mix	Turkey and Couscous	Strawberries with Balsamic Vinegar	1366
3	Fig and Ricotta Toast with Walnuts and Honey	Grilled Skirt Steak Over Hummus	Roasted Golden Beet and Watercress Salad	Chocolate and Avocado Mousse	1706
4	Banana Choco Breakfast Smoothie	Steamed Squash Chowder	Herbed Rice	Frozen Mango Raspberry Delight	1031
5	Spanish Toasted Tomato Baguettes	Pesto Chicken Pasta	Marinated Tuna Steak	Mango and Coconut Frozen Pie	1563
6	Breakfast Quinoa Muffins	Cod and Cauliflower Chowder	Lemon-Simmered Chicken & Artichokes	Crème Caramel	728
7	Herb-Encrusted Italian Omelet	Salmon and Couscous	Tarragon Cod Fillets	Triple Chocolate Tiramisu	846

Week 6

Days	Breakfast	Lunch	Dinner	Dessert	Total Kcal
1	Egg in A "Pepper Hole" With Avocado	Sautéed Kale with Tomato	Rosemary Pork Chops	Easy Strawberry Crepes Recipe	661
2	Cinnamon Apple and Lentils Porridge	Italian Minestrone	Tuna & Bean Wraps	Kourabiedes Almond Cookies	809
3	Harissa Shakshuka With Bell Peppers and Tomatoes	Braised Veal	Sesame Shrimp Mix	Raspberry Yogurt Basted Cantaloupe	838

Days	Breakfast	Lunch	Dinner	Dessert	Total Kcal
4	Mediterranean Breakfast Panini	Minty Balsamic Lamb	Salmon and Corn Salad	Apple and Berries Ambrosia	1353
5	Leeks and Eggs Muffins	Cheesy Tomato Salad	Sicilian Spaghetti	Easy Roasted Fruit Recipe	1108
6	Breakfast Yogurt Quinoa	Veggie Lo Mein	Roasted Lamb Chops	Pear Croustade	1400
7	Sun-Dried Tomatoes Oatmeal	Veggie Spaghetti	Cauliflower Tabbouleh Salad	Lemony Blackberry Granita	873

Week 7

Days	Breakfast	Lunch	Dinner	Dessert	Total Kcal
1	Fruity Breakfast Couscous	Sprouts of Alfalfa and Hummus	Baked Salmon with Garlic Cilantro Sauce	Mint Banana Chocolate Sorbet	1408
2	Fruity Yogurt-Topped Avocado Salad	Mango and Pasta Salad	Fennel and Walnuts Salad	Strawberries with Balsamic Vinegar	766
3	Fig and Ricotta Toast with Walnuts and Honey	Seasoned Beef Kebabs	Greek Lamb Burgers	Chocolate and Avocado Mousse	1699
4	Banana Choco Breakfast Smoothie	Shrimp with White Beans and Feta	Rice and Veggie Jambalaya	Frozen Mango Raspberry Delight	1434
5	Spanish Toasted Tomato Baguettes	Vegan Sesame Tofu and Eggplants	Pecorino Pasta with Sausage and Tomato	Mango and Coconut Frozen Pie	1595
6	Breakfast Quinoa Muffins	Maccheroni With Cherry Tomatoes and Anchovies	Calamari and Dill Sauce	Crème Caramel	991
7	Herb-Encrusted Italian Omelet	Mediterranean Spiced Lentils	Pork Chops and Herbed Tomato Sauce	Triple Chocolate Tiramisu	1052

Week 8

Days	Breakfast	Lunch	Dinner	Dessert	Total Kcal
1	Egg in A "Pepper Hole" With Avocado	Spanish Pepper Steak	Zucchini with Rice and Tzatziki	Easy Strawberry Crepes Recipe	1245
2	Cinnamon Apple and Lentils Porridge	Salmon and Peach Pan	Pork and Herbed Couscous Mix	Kourabiedes Almond Cookies	887.8

3	Harissa Shakshuka With Bell Peppers and Tomatoes	Roasted Eggplant and Chickpeas with Tomato Sauce	Walnut Turkey with Peaches	Raspberry Yogurt Basted Cantaloupe	1085
4	Mediterranean Breakfast Panini	Cucumber Olive Rice	Quick Vegetable Kebabs	Apple and Berries Ambrosia	1271
5	Leeks and Eggs Muffins	Chicken and Bow Tie Pasta	Garlic and Shrimp Pasta	Easy Roasted Fruit Recipe	1232.2
6	Breakfast Yogurt Quinoa	Salmon and Broccoli	Broccoli and Tomato Pasta	Pear Croustade	1404
7	Sun-Dried Tomatoes Oatmeal	Coriander and Coconut Chicken	Spanish Rice Casserole with Cheesy Beef	Lemony Blackberry Granita	1087

Week 9

Days	Breakfast	Lunch	Dinner	Dessert	Total Kcal
1	Apple Quinoa Breakfast Bars	Basil and Sun-Dried Tomatoes Rice	Cinnamon-Glazed Halibut Fillets	Revani Syrup Cake	1313
2	Egg in A "Pepper Hole" With Avocado	Couscous Pudding	Vegetarian Coconut Curry	Easy Roasted Fruit Recipe	936
3	Sun-Dried Tomatoes Oatmeal	Smoked Salmon and Watercress Salad	Greek Turkey Burger	Frozen Mango Raspberry Delight	912.7
4	Cinnamon Apple and Lentils Porridge	Ground Lamb with Lentils and Pomegranate Seeds	Radicchio and Smoked Bacon Risotto	Chocolate and Avocado Mousse	1656
5	Herb-Encrusted Italian Omelet	Italian White Bean Salad with Bell Peppers	Couscous and Apricots Bowls	Easy Strawberry Crepes Recipe	874
6	Fruity Breakfast Couscous	Cinnamon Couscous and Cauliflower	Chopped Tuna Salad	Strawberries with Balsamic Vinegar	990
7	Mediterranean Breakfast Panini	Baked Black-Eyed Peas	Sumac Chicken with Cauliflower and Carrots	Triple Chocolate Tiramisu	1671

Week 10

Days	Breakfast	Lunch	Dinner	Dessert	Total Kcal
1	Fruity Yogurt-Topped Avocado Salad	Crispy Mediterranean Chicken Thighs	Sweet Rice Pudding	Pear Croustade	1807

Days	Breakfast	Lunch	Dinner	Dessert	Total Kcal
2	Harissa Shakshuka With Bell Peppers and Tomatoes	White Wine–Sautéed Mussels	Spinach Pesto Pasta	Mango and Coconut Frozen Pie	1606
3	Banana Choco Breakfast Smoothie	Dill Cucumber Salad	Orange Duck and Celery	Mint Banana Chocolate Sorbet	989
4	Spanish Toasted Tomato Baguettes	Bean and Cabbage Soup	Flounder with Tomatoes and Basil	Raspberry Yogurt Basted Cantaloupe	641
5	Fig and Ricotta Toast with Walnuts and Honey	Delicious Chicken Pasta	Seared Scallops with Blood Orange Glaze	Lemony Blackberry Granita	1153
6	Breakfast Quinoa Muffins	Salmon and Radish Mix	Mediterranean Farfalle	Apple and Berries Ambrosia	1533.9
7	Apple Quinoa Breakfast Bars	Pork Tenderloin with Dill Sauce	Baked Mediterranean Rice	Revani Syrup Cake	1109

Week 11

Days	Breakfast	Lunch	Dinner	Dessert	Total Kcal
1	Fruity Breakfast Couscous	Lemon Mushroom Rice	Chicken Shawarma	Mint Banana Chocolate Sorbet	1245
2	Fruity Yogurt-Topped Avocado Salad	Cod and Mushrooms Mix	Turkey and Couscous	Strawberries with Balsamic Vinegar	1366
3	Fig and Ricotta Toast with Walnuts and Honey	Grilled Skirt Steak Over Hummus	Roasted Golden Beet and Watercress Salad	Chocolate and Avocado Mousse	1706
4	Banana Choco Breakfast Smoothie	Steamed Squash Chowder	Herbed Rice	Frozen Mango Raspberry Delight	1031
5	Spanish Toasted Tomato Baguettes	Pesto Chicken Pasta	Marinated Tuna Steak	Mango and Coconut Frozen Pie	1563
6	Breakfast Quinoa Muffins	Cod and Cauliflower Chowder	Lemon-Simmered Chicken & Artichokes	Crème Caramel	728
7	Herb-Encrusted Italian Omelet	Salmon and Couscous	Tarragon Cod Fillets	Triple Chocolate Tiramisu	846

Week 12

Days	Breakfast	Lunch	Dinner	Dessert	Total Kcal
1	Egg in A "Pepper Hole" With Avocado	Sautéed Kale with Tomato	Rosemary Pork Chops	Easy Strawberry Crepes Recipe	661
2	Cinnamon Apple and Lentils Porridge	Italian Minestrone	Tuna & Bean Wraps	Kourabiedes Almond Cookies	809
3	Harissa Shakshuka With Bell Peppers and Tomatoes	Braised Veal	Sesame Shrimp Mix	Raspberry Yogurt Basted Cantaloupe	838
4	Mediterranean Breakfast Panini	Minty Balsamic Lamb	Salmon and Corn Salad	Apple and Berries Ambrosia	1353
5	Leeks and Eggs Muffins	Cheesy Tomato Salad	Sicilian Spaghetti	Easy Roasted Fruit Recipe	1108
6	Breakfast Yogurt Quinoa	Veggie Lo Mein	Roasted Lamb Chops	Pear Croustade	1400
7	Sun-Dried Tomatoes Oatmeal	Veggie Spaghetti	Cauliflower Tabbouleh Salad	Lemony Blackberry Granita	873

Conclusion

The Mediterranean diet is more of a cultural eating pattern than a full-blown diet. Unlike nearly every popular diet, the Mediterranean diet isn't centered on what you can't eat. Rather, it focuses on how much you should eat and the type of things you should eat. Due to the area's geography, fish is a huge part of their diet. The climate of this area is also perfect for plant growth. Thanks to this, it's easier for those in this area to get fresh food than anything processed.

With fresh fruits and vegetables being within easy reach, these items make up a major portion of the diet. What isn't so easy to get a hold of in this area is red meat. Because of that, it is severely limited. White meats are included much more in this diet, but not as often as fish.

Finally, if you are an alcohol lover, you will like this! The Mediterranean diet includes wine. In fact, it's encouraged to have a glass with dinner. Just remember to keep it in moderation. The occasional glass of wine with dinner is included in this diet but beware of going overboard. Too much alcohol can quickly offset all the diet's benefits.

Another good news is that foods such as bread, pasta, and rice, which are often ruled out in other diets, are fine to eat on the Mediterranean Diet, as long as you opt for the wholegrain versions. These foods are staples in Mediterranean countries, and they're used to fill up, meaning you eat far less than you otherwise would, and you don't feel hungry a couple of hours later.

We hope you have found this book helpful and will continue to use it as a reference. The principles and guidelines found within this book can be adapted to fit any lifestyle. If you are still looking for ideas on how to put the Mediterranean diet into practice, we suggest you look into some of the recipes that are included.

Index

Almond Butter Banana Chocolate Smoothie; 75
Apple And Berries Ambrosia; 81
Apple Quinoa Breakfast Bars; 21
Avocado-Blueberry Smoothie; 75
Baked Black-Eyed Peas; 30
Baked Mediterranean Rice; 26
Baked Salmon with Garlic Cilantro Sauce; 51
Banana Choco Breakfast Smoothie; 21
Basil And Sun-Dried Tomatoes Rice; 24
Bean And Cabbage Soup; 24
Beef Cacciatore; 49
Blueberry Bananag; Protein: Smoothie; 74
Braised Veal; 45
Breakfast Quinoa Muffins; 17
Breakfast Yogurt Quinoa; 18
Broccoli And Tomato Pasta; 38
Calamari and Dill Sauce; 54
Cannellini Romesco Dip; 69
Cauliflower Tabbouleh Salad; 63
Cheesy Potato Mash; 64
Cheesy Tomato Salad; 62
Chia-Pomegranate Smoothie; 76
Chicken and Bow Tie Pasta; 32
Chicken Shawarma; 49
Chocolate And Avocado Mousse; 81
Chopped Tuna Salad; 55
Cinnamon Apple and Lentils Porridge; 17
Cinnamon Couscous And Cauliflower; 39
Cinnamon-Glazed Halibut Fillets; 57
Cod and Cauliflower Chowder; 54
Cod and Mushrooms Mix; 52
Confetti Couscous; 37
Coriander and Coconut Chicken; 48
Couscous And Apricots Bowls; 38
Couscous Pudding; 32
Cranberry-Pumpkin Smoothie; 74
Crème Caramel; 81
Crispy Mediterranean Chicken Thighs; 43
Cucumber Hummus Bites; 69
Cucumber Olive Rice; 25
Delicious Chicken Pasta; 36
Dill Cucumber Salad; 61
Dried Fruit Compote; 69
Easy Roasted Fruit Recipe; 78

Easy Strawberry Crepes Recipe; 78
Egg in a "Pepper Hole" with Avocado; 20
Fennel and Walnuts Salad; 62
Feta Artichoke Dip; 68
Fig and Ricotta Toast with Walnuts and Honey; 20
Flounder with Tomatoes and Basil; 55
Frozen Mango Raspberry Delight; 82
Fruit Smoothie; 74
Fruity Breakfast Couscous; 17
Fruity Yogurt-Topped Avocado Salad; 18
Garlic and Shrimp Pasta; 53
Greek Lamb Burgers; 43
Greek Turkey Burger; 47
Grilled Skirt Steak over Hummus; 42
Ground Lamb with Lentils and Pomegranate Seeds; 44
Harissa Shakshuka with Bell Peppers and Tomatoes; 19
Hearty Pear and Mango Smoothie; 73
Herbed Rice; 29
Herb-Encrusted Italian Omelet; 18
Honey And Wild Blueberry Smoothie; 73
Italian Minestrone; 34
Italian White Bean Salad with Bell Peppers; 62
Kale-Pineapple Smoothie; 73
Kourabiedes Almond Cookies; 79
Leeks and Eggs Muffins; 21
Lemon Mushroom Rice; 30
Lemon-Simmered Chicken & Artichokes; 43
Lemony Blackberry Granita; 80
Lentils and Cheddar Frittata; 70
Loukoumades (Fried Honey Balls); 67
Maccheroni With Cherry Tomatoes And Anchovies; 36
Mango And Coconut Frozen Pie; 79
Mango And Pasta Salad; 33
Mango-Pear Smoothie; 76
Marinated Tuna Steak; 53
Mediterranean Breakfast Panini; 17
Mediterranean Farfalle; 40
Mediterranean Smoothie; 76
Mediterranean Spiced Lentils; 28
Mint Banana Chocolate Sorbet; 79
Minty Balsamic Lamb; 45

Moroccan Avocado Smoothie; 74
Oats Berry Smoothie; 73
Orange Duck and Celery; 48
Peanut Butter Banana Greek Yogurt; 75
Pear Croustade; 82
Pecorino Pasta With Sausage And Tomato; 35
Pesto Chicken Pasta; 32
Pork And Herbed Couscous Mix; 37
Pork Chops and Herbed Tomato Sauce; 46
Pork Tenderloin with Dill Sauce; 47
Prosciutto Wrapped Plums; 70
Pumpkin-Spiced Quinoa; 71
Quick Vegetable Kebabs; 65
Radicchio And Smoked Bacon Risotto; 27
Raspberry Vanilla Smoothie; 75
Raspberry Yogurt Basted Cantaloupe; 80
Revani Syrup Cake; 83
Rice And Veggie Jambalaya; 26
Roasted Eggplant and Chickpeas with Tomato Sauce; 64
Roasted Golden Beet and Watercress Salad; 63
Roasted Lamb Chops; 48
Rosemary Pork Chops; 42
Salmon and Broccoli; 56
Salmon and Corn Salad; 51
Salmon And Couscous; 35
Salmon and Peach Pan; 56
Salmon and Radish Mix; 58
Salmon Rolls; 71
Sautéed Kale with Tomato; 61
Savory Greek White Fava Beans; 29
Seared Scallops with Blood Orange Glaze; 57
Seasoned Beef Kebabs; 42
Sesame Shrimp Mix; 51
Shrimp with White Beans and Feta; 52
Sicilian Spaghetti; 37
Simple Tuna Pasta; 39
Smoked Salmon and Watercress Salad; 56
Spanish Pepper Steak; 45
Spanish Rice Casserole With Cheesy Beef; 28
Spanish Toasted Tomato Baguettes; 22
Spicy Watermelon Mango Salsa; 67
Spinach Pesto Pasta; 34
Sprouts Of Alfalfa And Hummus; 24
Steamed Squash Chowder; 60
Stewed Okra; 60
Strawberries With Balsamic Vinegar; 80
Stuffed Avocado; 67
Sumac Chicken with Cauliflower and Carrots; 46
Sun-Dried Tomatoes Oatmeal; 20
Sweet Rice Pudding; 25
Tarragon Cod Fillets; 57
Tomato Bruschetta; 68
Tomato Salsa; 70
Triple Chocolate Tiramisu; 82
Tuna & Bean Wraps; 55
Turkey And Couscous; 39
Vegan Sesame Tofu and Eggplants; 61
Vegetarian Coconut Curry; 60
Veggie Lo Mein; 65
Veggie Spaghetti; 33
Vinegar Beet Bites; 70
Walnut Turkey with Peaches; 47
Watermelon And Blueberry Salad; 68
White Wine–Sautéed Mussels; 54
Zucchini With Rice And Tzatziki; 27

Made in United States
Orlando, FL
13 May 2023

MEDITERRANEAN DIET COOKBOOK FOR BEGINNERS

Countless Easy and Tasty Recipes to Quickly Build your Healthy Habits, Help Shed Weight, and Feel Lighter Every Day. Boost your Well-Being with the 12-Week Meal Plan

MELINDA JEFFERSON

Copyright ©2023 by Melinda Jefferson. All rights reserved.

MEDITERRANEAN DIET COOKBOOK FOR BEGINNERS

ISBN: ISBN: 979-8391401469

10 9 8 7 6 5 4 3 2 1

All rights reserved